almonds,
anchovies,
&
pancetta

Also by Cal Peternell

Twelve Recipes

A Recipe for Cooking

almonds, anchovies, + pancetta

A VEGETARIAN COOKBOOK, KIND OF

CAL PETERNELL

WM
WILLIAM MORROW
An Imprint of HarperCollins*Publishers*

ALMONDS, ANCHOVIES, AND PANCETTA. Copyright © 2018 by Cal Peternell. All rights reserved. Printed in China. No part of this book may be used or reproduced in any manner whatsoever without written permission except in the case of brief quotations embodied in critical articles and reviews. For information, address HarperCollins Publishers, 195 Broadway, New York, NY 10007.

HarperCollins books may be purchased for educational, business, or sales promotional use. For information, please email the Special Markets Department at SPsales@harpercollins.com.

FIRST EDITION

Designed by Suet Yee Chong
Illustrations by Milo Henderson, Liam Peternell, Kathleen Henderson, and Cal Peternell

Library of Congress Cataloging-in-Publication Data has been applied for.

ISBN 978-0-06-274743-3

18 19 20 21 22   IM   10 9 8 7 6 5 4 3 2 1

For Liam, Milo, and Henderson

You three make life for me very much better

than almonds, anchovies, and even pancetta!

My favorite meals are cooked, and eaten, together with you.

contents

introduction

The way I like to eat today is the same way people have been eating forever: vegetables at center-plate seasoned with a little bit of meat or fish to make it savory and satisfying. All over the world, we love, for example, the way a smoky ham hock does good things for a pot of beans or skillet of greens, how chicken stock gets slowly pulled into simmering rice, how shavings of bonito brine our broths. A little of the right kind of meat goes a long way. There are many right kinds, but in this book, the right ones are anchovies and pancetta, and, because nuts are the meat of the plant world, I've added the fatty and flavorful almond, a kindred spirit. (Other kinds of nuts, as well as varieties of cured pork and fishes, are in here too—substituting, say, walnuts for almonds, bottarga for anchovies, or bacon for pancetta is encouraged.) It's a *kind* of vegetarian diet, eaten by those of us who love vegetables so much that we sometimes honor them with small gifts, bringing offerings of toasted nuts, of salted fishes, and of sweet cured pork bellies.

I cook this way first for the flavor, but also because it makes sense: in a crowded world full of eaters, taking savory little bites is inarguably better than big meaty mouthfuls. It's healthy, leans toward sustainability, and is economical in a way that pleases both palate and pocketbook. And when that grilled steak, roasted chicken, or fried fish fillet does come along, I enjoy it all the more.

In a way, this cookbook, and so much in cooking, is really about one ingredient: salt. Salt draws out and enhances flavors, but it also preserves. Anchovies and pancetta, cured for the savoriest of eating, would not exist without salt. Nor would other staples-turned-delicacies like baccalà, kimchi, sauerkraut, lox, olives, capers, Parmesan, prosciutto, bresaola, biltong, or umeboshi. One need not scrape too deeply beneath the crystalline crust of the history of salt-preserved foods to learn that they are ultimately peasant foods, invented to keep excess seasonal harvests from spoiling. Though few of us cure our own meats, fishes, and vegetables these days, we have evolved culinarily to crave them. There is even a certain pride shown in the enjoyment of cured foods, a bravado that comes from the way that salt can amplify a food's essential funkiness and render it funkier still, like Bootsy thumping hard on the bass.

Almonds aren't just tagging along here—just like panc- etta and anchovies, they can be added in small amounts to bring a flavor boost to a dish. They compare fa- vorably fat-wise and deliver similar umami levels, especially when ground up. Almonds can also be used in larger amounts, in desserts of course, but also in savory sauces, soups hot or cold, and to en- rich stews. If you prefer to eat only plants, this is your ingredient (but don't ignore the other sections— the anchovies and pancetta can, if they must, be easily left out of many of the recipes).

I admire the conviction of those who do their cooking and make their feasts using only plants. Just like the finest and freshest vegetables, vegetarians don't *need* anchovies, fish sauce, bacon, or pancetta, but sometimes I wonder if they might *want* some. When, for example, stalks of spring asparagus are just so, you should, by all means, cook them as simply as possi- ble, if at all, to eat straight, with a little salt and olive oil. Another time, try them tossed with sizzled sage and pancetta, say, or almonds. Vegetables of every sort and of all seasons deserve to be brought up a notch with judi- cious additions of one, or more, of the trio. Taste your sautéed summer peppers or sim- mered autumn greens and see if they don't

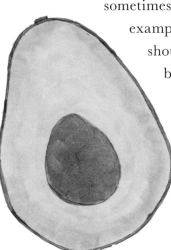

want a little anchovy or pancetta melted in. Deep in winter, make squashes crunchy with almonds, roasted roots rich with pancetta, and bittersweet chicories pungent with anchovies.

Eat lots of vegetables to stay healthy, and give them a savory fishy, nutty, or porky boost to keep happy.

HOW TO USE THIS COOKBOOK

The best cooking begins with the best ingredients, no way around it. If you think you can't tell the difference between season-less produce that has made its way from factory farm to vast supermarket and in-season stuff from a local farm, or that you grew yourself, I think you are not giving yourself enough credit: You absolutely can! It doesn't mean that you shouldn't cook with whatever you've got right now—you should, of course—but that it is very much worth it to seek out better meats, dairy, produce, everything, for next time. I encourage you further to substitute other varieties of a particular vegetable for the one called for in my recipe, and indeed to substitute other vegetables entirely if they seem better at the market. The green beans don't look great but the snap peas do? Switch them out. I ask for Persian cucumbers, but your store's only got English? Totally fine.

Some of the recipes here—pastas, salads, appetizers—can stand alone. You know what to do with those. Many others can play their traditional roles on the plate alongside fish or meat, but I often will cook several "sides" and serve them together to make a meal—sometimes with rice, polenta, or a good loaf of bread. For example:

Sweet Corn with Almonds and Sage, page 40

&

Grilled Pancetta-Wrapped Figs Smashed on Toast,
page 133

Green Bean and Frisée Salad with Almond
and Anchovy Dressing, page 81

&

Bacon-Wrapped Potato Gratin, page 149

Artichokes and New Onions Baked with Anchovies
and Bread Crumbs, page 70

&

Buttered Peas with Pancetta, Lettuce, and Sage, page 122

Creamy White Beans with Pancetta and Rosemary, page 165

&

Thick Toast with Kale, Cardoons, Garlic, and Anchovies, page 76

Tonnato Sauce on sliced tomatoes, page 95

&

Green Beans with Shallots, Basil, and Almonds,
page 27

Bacon-Wrapped Potato Gratin, page 149

&

Snap Peas Amandine, page 26

Cauliflower with Almond Aillade, page 56

&

*Greens with Big Chunks of Braised Pancetta and
Garlic Cloves, page 143*

Creamy White Beans with Pancetta and Rosemary, page 165

&

*Celery and Apple Salad with Pounded Almonds, Anchovies, Parmesan,
and Parsley, page 51*

ON POUNDING GARLIC AND ANCHOVIES

First, a request: get a mortar and pestle, please. (A good size one, about five inches across, preferably made of olive wood or gran-ite. They don't cost much and never wear out, though I had a mortar made of lesser wood that absorbed too much garlic and so on and started to go a bit rogue after a while. I set it free.) For pounding garlic, anchovies, or almonds, your mortar and pestle's the thing.

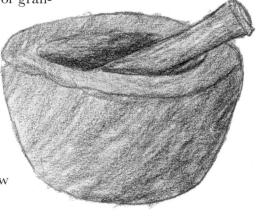

Garlic: Sprinkling a pinch of salt on a raw

garlic clove before pounding helps it to become a liquid-y paste—what you want when you're adding raw garlic to vinaigrettes, pesto and other green sauces, raita, aïoli, and so on. (For reference, my "pinch" of salt is the equivalent of a quarter of a quarter-teaspoon. I measured it for you, reader: four pinches fill a quarter-teaspoon measure.) Garlic can be pounded with salt in a mortar and pestle, or, if you've ignored my request, on a cutting board with a chef's knife like this: place the garlic clove on a cutting board, put the flat side of the knife atop it, and smack the knife hard with your hand. Sprinkle the crushed clove with salt, and crush it again. Chop the garlic holding the tip of the knife down and using a paper-cutter motion. When lots of sticky garlic clings to the knife, smear it sideways so it stays on the board. Continue crushing, chopping, and smearing until the garlic and salt have turned almost liquid.

Anchovies: Whatever you're making with the anchovies, chances are that you'll be combining them with garlic. If so, pound the anchovies right on top of the garlic already mashed up in the mortar. If you're using a knife on a cutting board, perform the crush-chop-smear technique, just as for garlic, but without the initial hard smack and without adding salt.

For years I cooked with kosher salt, though now I prefer to use fine sea salt. It has a better, more natural feel and taste, but when I am on vacation and forget to pack a bag of it, I use kosher. Other than on popcorn, I never use table salt if I can help it.

Whenever my dad spies on me in the kitchen, he comments on my persistent salting "You use a lot of salt, don't you?" he says.

I should probably just say "Yeah, I guess so" or "Not that much, really," but instead it's "I use the *right* amount."

Snotty, I know, but it's true: I use the amount that tastes right to me. That's what you (and my dad) should do, too. Too often, though, I see people adding salt as if it were ritual, not flavoring. They'll

sprinkle, with the dainty tips of their thumb and forefinger, a quantity of grains so small as to be entirely ineffective, unless you are seasoning nothing more than one bite of an egg, say, or a wee radish. For scooping up salt to add to pasta- or vegetable-cooking water, for example, you're going to need to use at least a thumb-plus-three-fingers pinch, and you should taste the water before any food goes in to determine if you've got it right—it should be pleasantly seasoned, the way you'd want a spoonful of soup to taste.

ON OILS

I use my best-tasting extra-virgin olive oil in vinaigrettes and other places where it's to be eaten raw. Though one could use the same oil for cooking, it makes more sense to have a less expensive oil on hand, either regular olive oil or a vegetable oil or a combination of the two. In these recipes, I refer to the first as good olive oil and the second as cooking oil.

almonds

You know, almonds are a good snack; I strongly
recommend them.
— *Barack Obama, President of the United States of America*

I miss President Obama.

He was smart, literate, eloquent, and sensible. Questioning whether he
was born in the United States, that's just plain racist of course, but I have
wondered about those seven almonds he would eat as he read late into the
night (as opposed to tweeting early in the morning). What was that about?
He did say he might up the nightly snack count once out of office. Wild man!

In fact, Mr. President, almonds are more than a snack. Consider
the nutty and surprisingly contemporary ancient Greek story of Agdistis to get a sense of the almond's potency: Cybele, the Phyrgian Earth-
Mother, aka Gaia, had long been putting off Zeus's unwanted attentions,

but even Earth-Mother has to sleep sometime. In crept horny Zeus, who did his thing onto the fertility goddess's sleeping body, and, just like that, baby Agdistis was conceived. Agdistis was born a hermaphrodite—not a problem—until the gods didn't like it, fearing that her intersex body gave her too much power. The paranoid plan they came up with was to cut off her penis and bury it in the ground. Done, they thought. Never one to be kept down, the penis grew into a sturdy and glorious almond tree. By and by, Nana, the nymph daughter of the river-god Sangarius, strolled beneath its branches and picked an almond from the penis-tree and put it between her breasts. Naturally. Unnaturally, Nana became pregnant. Her child Attis grew up handsome and hot, and who falls in love with him? Agdistis! See what I'm talking about?!

I was a kid, making chocolate chip cookies, the first time I ever tasted what I thought was an almond. I reached into my mom's kitchen cabinet and grabbed the wrong bottle of imitation: The "almond" extract was sitting right next to the "vanilla" extract. It was as I tipped the chemically potent liquor from bottle to teaspoon that I noticed my mistake. The aroma I inhaled through my ten-year-old nose provoked a nostalgia for things that hadn't happened yet. I had memories of times to come when I'd eat flaky pastries fragrant with frangipane in ornate Florentine bars, and a cold breakfast of almond granita in a hot Sicilian summer café; memories of callison: almond candies like ivory tiles that I would eat at Chez Panisse so many years later and feel that they maybe were my namesake sweet; memories of Márquez and the scent of bitter almonds and unrequited love. Smell memories can be that powerful. Synthetic benzaldehyde, the bottled stuff that was in Mom's kitchen, may be so powerful that it can take you back to the future.

Now, of course, I cook with whole organic almonds. Not because I have a point to make other than that they taste better, and *are* better. They won't get anyone pregnant but they do have a high fat content (the good kind) and an inherent sweetness. They are toasty when roasted and, when ground fine, can enrich and thicken soups and stews.

Almonds have the endorsement of chefs, of at least one great president, and of the gods.

TIPS FOR TOASTING, CHOPPING, AND BLANCHING NUTS, SEEDS, AND SPICES

People who know me as a cook—that is, fellow pro cooks and pretty much anyone who has ever been to my house—know that I like to use a kitchen timer. Some of my kitchenmates have been shocked by it, and I suspect there are many who feel needled and annoyed by an interruptive *brrrrrrrring!* or *beepity-beep!,* but a nice wind-up timer sets *me* free. Ticking away reassuringly, my Minute Minder does just what its name promises so that I can get as distracted as I need to and still not burn the toast. The timer in my kitchen has very distinct purposes—of course I would never use it to tell me when to turn the steak on the grill or when pasta or vegetables are done boiling—the best tools for that are our built-in senses: sound, touch, and especially taste. But when cookies, nuts, or bread crumbs are toasting out of sight in the oven, when an egg is boiling or a bottle of white wine needs to be quickly chilled but not blow-the-top frozen, I twist up my timer.

At some point you will say *toast, schmoast* and just use your almonds raw. We've all done it and maybe you should just go ahead and do it now and get it over with. You'll see that it would be much nicer if the nuts were crunchy instead of soft, if the flavor were more robust, if they were a bit sweeter. Sometimes very fresh nuts are the exception, tasting sweet and crisp just like that. Otherwise, toast.

To toast almonds or other nuts, heat the oven to 350°F. Spread the nuts on a baking sheet, put them in the oven, and set the timer for 8 minutes. Bite or cut a nut in half—it should be tan inside but won't be crisp yet; that will happen when it cools. If it needs more time, give it more, resetting the timer. Let the nuts cool. Often the skins are tannic and sawdusty; to remove them, swaddle the nuts in a clean kitchen towel and roll them around in a meatball-making motion. Some of the skins will resist your effort and that's okay.

To toast whole spices, such as cumin, coriander, or fennel, heat a dry skillet to medium and add the seeds. When they start to hop around a little and smell spicy, shake the pan and toast for 15 seconds. Use spices whole, crushed, or ground fine.

To toast sesame seeds, heat a dry skillet to medium and add the seeds in a shallow layer—if there are too many in the skillet they won't toast evenly. Shake the skillet and stir or toss the seeds as they toast. When they begin to pop, turn off the heat and continue to toast over residual heat until the seeds are golden brown.

Chopping nuts with a knife can be tricky: they keep rolling away from you, especially almonds and hazelnuts. One pro tip is to first crush them with a rolling pin and then either knife-chop them, or just keep rolling until they are the texture you desire.

Blanching nuts: They say that cooks are divided into two groups: those who love to blanch and peel almonds and those who despair of the task. Maybe, but it's not a lifetime membership—I have witnessed conversions and expect to see more. There can be satisfactions disproportionate to the size of the tasks, and sitting around squeezing the brown husky skin off almonds is one of those tasks. The almonds are warm and damp and when the skin pops right off to reveal the pale nude nut beneath, you just sigh. Work in groups; we all need more satisfaction.

Almonds can be peeled raw and then toasted, or vice versa. Either way, bring a saucepan of water to a boil. The skins will slip right off most satisfyingly while the almonds are still hot out of the water, so do them in batches: drop a small handful into the boiling water and fish them out after half a minute. As soon as you can handle them, squeeze each almond to slip the skin off. If the skin sticks, dip the offender back in the water to loosen it. Discard the skins.

CARROT AND ALMOND SOUP WITH SAFFRON AND CORIANDER

Every chef I know likes to make soup, and I'm no exception. I, however, have something no one else has, a secret advantage: My souper power is my son Liam, an enthusiast with an appetite so potent that he alone can drive demand, inspiration, and production. And it's not just the cooking; I love everything about feeding him soup: spoon on the proper side for a lefty, DNA-embedded satisfaction of ladle-to-bowl motion, sweet sounds of son's slurping. Even when he would arrive after school and hungry at Chez Panisse, he'd walk right past the pastry sirens with their chocolate pavés and raspberry coulis to sit at the bowl of soup I'd set out for him. Half a loaf of buttered fendu clutched in one hand, he'd get to determined spooning with the other. Of course chocolate and raspberry frivolities followed, the perks of restaurant familyhood, but I liked him fed and starting in on homework in his little corner of the dining room first.

Makes 2 quarts, about 8 servings

¼ cup cooking oil, olive or vegetable

1 medium yellow onion, thinly sliced

Kosher or sea salt

½ teaspoon saffron threads (about 10 threads)

1½ pounds carrots, peeled and cut in approximately ½-inch chunks

½ cup toasted, peeled (nice, but optional, see page 14), roughly crushed almonds

1½ teaspoons white wine vinegar

2 teaspoons coriander seeds,
toasted (see page 14)

3 tablespoons good olive oil

Marash, Urfa, Aleppo, or other
dried and crushed mild red pepper
to taste

Heat a soup pot over high heat. Add the oil and then the onion, ½ teaspoon salt, and the saffron. Stir, lower the heat, and cover the pot. Check and stir after a few minutes, letting water from the lid drip back into the pot to keep things steamy. Lower the heat if there is any browning going on, re-cover, and cook like this, stirring occasionally, until very tender, about 15 minutes. Add the carrots, almonds, another ½ teaspoon salt and enough water to cover the carrots by about an inch. You can always thin the soup later if it's too thick, so add just enough water to allow the carrots to bob around a bit. Bring to a boil over high heat, then lower to an easy simmer, stirring occasionally to prevent sticking. Cook until the carrots are very tender, about 30 minutes. If the carrots are undercooked, the texture of the soup won't be as nice: You should be able to spoon-crush a carrot chunk against the side of the pot.

Unless you're in a hurry, let the soup cool, at least a little, before blending— it's safer. Stir in the vinegar and puree the soup in batches at the most annoying blender speed until you can't take it. Pass the soup through a sieve for extra smoothness, re-blending with the next batch what got caught in the sieve from the previous one if you are economical like me. Taste and adjust the soup for salt and acidity. Adjust the texture with water—it should be pleasantly thick, but with flow. A spoon should leave no enduring sign of its passing, and remember that the soup will thicken further as it cools in the bowl.

Grind the coriander seeds finely, but not quite to powder, and stir them together with the olive oil and a pinch of salt. Reheat the soup as needed, ladle into warm bowls, and spoon the coriander oil on top. Sprinkle with Marash or other pepper as desired.

AJO BLANCO

You get all kinds in restaurant dining rooms. After fairly fuming over endless dietary requests over the years, I have become more sanguine about them—I figure everybody has their food thing, and for all sorts of reasons, so it's best to not question and just go with it. Occasionally, though, you come up against one that you can't quite bring yourself to accommodate—the guest is asking that you put each course: the salad, pasta, and grilled lamb, tapenade, potato gratin, and watercress, in the blender and serve like a series of smoothies? Um, no.

There is, however, one salad that I do like to blitz in a blender: gazpacho. I know, it's a soup, but I build it like a salad, tossing all the ingredients in a big bowl with a couple handfuls of ice, dressing it with oil and vinegar till it tastes right, and then spinning the heck out of the whole thing.

I make ajo blanco, a tomato-less proto-gazpacho, this way, too. I like ajo blanco with a lot of garlic, so the best time to make it is as soon as the cucumbers arrive at markets in the late spring, when the garlic is still fresh and not too intense. Since really good grapes, the traditional garnish, tend to show up later in the summer, I sometimes use early, sweet melon instead. Ajo blanco can be made all summer long, of course, just use a lighter hand with the garlic as it gets stronger.

1 cup almonds, toasted (see page 14)

1 cup torn, crustless white bread

2 medium cucumbers, peeled and sliced

2 scallions or 1 spring onion, all the white and most of the green parts, thinly sliced

1 or several garlic cloves, pounded (see page 6)

2 teaspoons sherry vinegar

¼ cup good olive oil, plus a little for drizzling on top of the soup

½ teaspoon kosher or sea salt

6 to 8 ice cubes

1 small ripe green melon, peeled, seeded, and cut into bite-size cubes (Piel de Sapo is a favorite. Honeydew, too.)

6 mint leaves, thinly sliced

Bring a saucepan of water to a boil for boiling and peeling the almonds. The skins will slip right off most satisfyingly while the almonds are still hot out of the water, so work in batches: drop a small handful into the boiling water and fish them out after a minute. As soon as you can handle them, squeeze each almond to slip the skin off. If the skin sticks, dip the offender back in the water to loosen it. Discard the skins.

Tear the bread into a large mixing bowl. Add the cucumbers, almonds, scallions or spring onion, garlic, vinegar, olive oil, and salt. Add the ice cubes, stir well to get the juices going, and refrigerate for 20 to 30 minutes to marinate and chill. Puree the soup in the blender, in batches if necessary and adding little splashes of water as needed to get it going. Pass through a strainer for a silkier texture, taste, adjust, and serve cold, scattered with cubes of melon and slivers of mint, and drizzled with olive oil.

CUCUMBERS AND MELON WITH SPICY ALMOND CROCCANTE, CILANTRO, BASIL, AND SCALLIONS

The pastry cooks at Chez Panisse have a big marble slab built right into their counter. I was always kind of jealous of the marble—it looked pretty fun rolling out hot nougat, scraping up thin chocolate curls, and spreading almond croccante that always seemed to spontaneously form itself into the map-shape of France. Croccante (say: croak-*on*-tay) is like almond brittle, thin and crisp, and bittersweet. It's good to crush over ice cream, or mix into cookie dough, or just crunch on. I added lots of black and red pepper to my savory version of croccante pretty much just so I could use that cool marble. Here it spikes a salad of melon and its summer cousin cucumber.

Makes enough for the salad and more (store in a jar with a tight lid)

Croccante

Cooking oil, olive or vegetable

1½ cups sugar

2 cups sliced almonds

1½ teaspoons freshly ground black pepper

½ teaspoon crushed red pepper flakes

¾ teaspoon kosher or sea salt

Painted Serpent Cucumber

Salad

½ teaspoon grated or finely chopped ginger

Juice of ½ lime

½ teaspoon white wine vinegar

Kosher or sea salt

3 tablespoons good olive oil

3 or 4 scallions, all the white and most of the green parts, thinly sliced

Half of the most delicious ripe melon (the other half is for breakfast tomorrow)

1 cucumber, peeled

1 loose cup basil leaves (about 6 sprigs)

1 loose cup cilantro leaves (about 8 sprigs)

Make the croccante: Brush a baking sheet with oil, and oil a same-size sheet of parchment paper. Have a rolling pin handy.

In a heavy-bottomed saucepan, combine the sugar and 2 tablespoons water and cook over medium-high heat. The sugar will melt and begin to look like a frozen tundra before turning light brown around the edges. You can stir, or nudge, it around with a wooden spoon to help the caramel along. Eventually it will turn to liquid caramel that is light brown, getting browner, and very hot, so please be careful. Turn off the heat when it is, well, caramel colored. You want it to be bittersweet, so let it get pretty dark, but not burned-black, and remember that it will keep cooking a little, even after the heat is off.

Add the almonds, black pepper, red pepper flakes, and salt, and mix them in very well, standing back a little to avoid the sneezy pepper fumes. Turn the mixture out onto the prepared baking sheet, lay the oiled parchment on it (oil side down), and spread it as thinly as possible with the rolling pin. Let the croccante cool completely, eat some, use some for the salad, and store anything that's leftover in an airtight container for later.

To make the dressing, stir together the ginger, lime juice, vinegar, ¼ teaspoon salt, and the olive oil. Stir in the scallions and set aside.

With a soup spoon, scoop the seeds out of the melon and discard. Use the spoon to scoop out bite-size chunks of melon and put them in a big mixing bowl. Cut the ends off the cucumber, split it in half lengthwise, and cut the halves into random chunks the size of the melon chunks. Add the basil and cilantro leaves, a sprinkle of salt, and most of the dressing. Toss to coat well, taste, adjust, and spread onto a platter. Drizzle with the remaining dressing. Crumble, chop, or crush some of the croccante and sprinkle on top. Not too much—make them beg for more.

Variation: There's another way to make the candied almond part of this salad. Done this way, the almonds are even more irresistible—addictive to the point that I felt some reluctance to share it. But you can handle it; you won't start eating bowlfuls with milk for breakfast, won't end up with little bits of it in your pockets, won't think about it everywhere all day. It's actually slightly easier to make, sorry. The recipe is on the next page, but maybe you should tear it out and destroy it now.

SPICY ALMOND CRACK

Makes 2 cups

¼ cup sugar

2 cups raw sliced almonds

½ teaspoon kosher or sea salt

¼ teaspoon crushed red pepper flakes

Freshly ground black pepper

Heat the oven to 325°F. In a small saucepan, combine the sugar with ¼ cup water and bring to a boil over this page as it burns. Just kidding, do it on the stove over high heat, swirling occasionally until the sugar is completely melted. Place the almonds in a mixing bowl with the salt and crushed red pepper flakes and crank in a lot of black pepper. Pour the sugar syrup over the almonds and stir well, stepping back to avoid the volatile steam. Place the almonds in a sieve set over a bowl and let drain for 5 minutes. Spread the drained almonds onto a baking sheet in a single-ish layer and bake, stirring after 10 minutes, until golden brown, 15 to 20 minutes total. Let cool completely. Dangerously good to serve with drinks. Keep in a jar with a tight (locked?) lid.

ALMOND BUTTER AND
CUCUMBER SANDWICHES WITH SHALLOTS

All of my recipes are personal, but some feel private—this is one of those. Not a dirty shame thing, like hoovering down corporate cheesy chili chips, metal cranked up, smoke still in the air. Private, as in: This is a sandwich I came up with hungry, and from a sparse pantry, that turned out so comforting and specific, a bespoke pleasure, the ASMR of snacks. I have never made these little sandwiches with anyone watching. Never done the thing with the chips, either; there are simply times when one likes to eat alone.

Makes enough to hoard for yourself or share with one friend

1 small shallot

Kosher or sea salt

Sherry vinegar

2 thin slices whole grain bread

3 to 4 tablespoons almond butter

1 small cucumber (Persians are perfect), or half a regular slicer

Marash or other mild red pepper flakes (Urfa, Aleppo, or similar) to taste

Slice the shallot as thinly as possible and dress it with a pinch of salt and a moistening of sherry vinegar. Set aside while you lightly toast the bread. Spread the toasts with the almond butter. Slice the cucumber thinly and arrange atop the almond butter. Sprinkle with salt, Marash pepper, and the sliced shallot. Leave open-faced or not. Call a friend?

SNAP PEAS AMANDINE

Why not give sweet snap peas the royal treatment, as if they were fine fillets of Dover sole? Is it rich? Yes. Do you have to be? Nope.

Makes 6 servings

Kosher or sea salt

1 pound snap peas, stems and strings removed

6 tablespoons (¾ stick) unsalted butter

½ cup sliced almonds, toasted (see page 14)

2 strips lemon peel, no pith, slivered crosswise very thinly

1 tablespoon chopped parsley

Freshly ground black pepper

Bring a pot of salted water to a boil for the snap peas and heat a skillet over medium-low for the almond-butter sauce—they will take about the same time to cook. Add the snap peas to the water and the butter to the skillet. The butter will melt, foam, and sizzle, and just when it begins to brown, add the sliced almonds and a pinch of salt and stir for 15 seconds. Add the lemon peel and parsley, stir, and add the drained snap peas if they are done (tender, but not falling apart) and a splash of water to mix with the butter. If the snap peas aren't done yet, splash a little water into the skillet and lower the heat to slow it down while they finish. Stir to coat the snap peas well and grind in black pepper to taste.

GREEN BEANS WITH SHALLOTS, BASIL, AND ALMONDS

You never forget the first time you went full herbal. It was sweet and soon you just couldn't seem to get enough of the green, fragrant leaf. Basil is what I'm talking about (what were you thinking?) and my first time was with pesto, some say basil's apex state. I immediately wanted to live there. Before, herbs were things I *didn't* eat: curly parsley borders at brunch or dusty jars on a long, long Lazy Susan ride. These days, my kitchen counters are positively green from parsley chopping sessions and herb picking is a fragrant, nightly, pre-dinner ritual at which refreshments are served. And even when I am not making pesto, I still like to cook with handfuls of basil, sautéing it to set the color and infuse the oil with flavor.

Makes 6 servings

Kosher or sea salt

¼ cup cooking oil, olive or vegetable

1 large shallot (or half a small red onion), thinly sliced

1 pound green beans, stem ends snapped off

1 generous cup basil leaves, very roughly chopped

¼ cup almonds, toasted (see page 14) and roughly chopped or crushed

Bring a pot of water to a boil and add salt till it tastes right (see page 8).

When the water is boiling, heat a skillet to medium and add the oil and then the shallot and a pinch of salt. Stir. Add the green beans to the pot. When the shallot has browned slightly and is softened but with a little crunch, add the basil leaves to the skillet and stir for 30 seconds. Stir in the almonds and, when they're tender, drain the green beans and add them. Taste one to be sure—if they need another minute, splash a little water into the skillet and lower the heat so it will wait for them. Stir, taste, and adjust.

Variation: Add 1 cup chopped ripe tomatoes to the skillet with the cooked shallot, basil, and almonds. Add a little salt and cook over medium heat just until the tomatoes lose their rawness, about 3 minutes. Add ⅓ cup cream and bring to a simmer. Add the boiled green beans, toss, taste, and adjust.

PAN-ROASTED EGGPLANT SALAD
WITH PEANUT AND HOT RED PEPPER SAUCE

Cooking eggplant can be tricky. The mistake is often in undercooking, but I think I've come up with a solution: Cook eggplant slices *al mattone* style! That is, under some sort of weight that will press the surface of the slices flat to the skillet. Not only does this ensure more even browning, but it also creates an ad hoc oven that helps to cook the eggplant through. *Mattone* means brick, but unless you are using a brick-shaped skillet to cook in, a pot or pan just smaller around than your skillet will fit best. Wrap the business side of your *mattone*, whether brick or pan, with foil to keep things tidy.

Makes 6 servings

2 globe eggplants (about 2 pounds)

Kosher or sea salt

Cooking oil, olive or vegetable

½ cup roasted peanuts (see page 14 to roast your own), crushed and/or chopped

½ teaspoon cumin seeds, toasted (see page 14) and ground

1 almond-size garlic clove, pounded (see page 6)

3 tablespoons sambal oelek (or other favorite red chile paste)

2 tablespoons finely julienned, peeled ginger

2 or 3 scallions, all the white and most of the green parts, trimmed and thinly sliced

½ cup picked cilantro leaves

Using a vegetable peeler, take lengthwise strips of skin from the eggplants, so that they are striped. Cut across into ½-inch-thick rounds and sprinkle them with about a teaspoon of salt. Heat a skillet to medium, then add 3 table-spoons oil and as many eggplant slices as will fit in a single layer. Tilt the skillet to distribute the oil and place a slightly smaller, foil-wrapped skillet atop the slices. Peek at one of the slices after a couple of minutes to see that it's not browning too little or too much and adjust the heat accordingly. When nicely browned, about 5 minutes, turn to do the other side and replace the top skillet. When tender—a knife tip will slip in with no resistance—set the eggplant aside, add more oil, and cook the remaining slices. You can keep them warm in the oven or leave them to eat at room temperature.

While the eggplant cooks, make the peanut and chili sauce: In a small bowl, mix the peanuts, cumin, garlic, sambal oelek, a pinch of salt, and 3 tablespoons oil. Stir well, taste, adjust, and set aside.

When the eggplant slices are done, keep the skillet warm and add another tablespoon of oil and then the ginger. Fry over low heat until beginning to brown lightly, then stir the ginger into the peanut sauce.

Put the eggplant slices on a platter, spoon the sauce on top, and scatter with the scallions and cilantro leaves. Nice with sliced tomatoes tucked among the eggplant and boiled rice.

ALMOND AND RED PEPPER MUHAMMARA

As a teenager, I read a lot, believing I could find in books something I was missing in rural New Jersey. I dove especially deep into Vladimir Nabokov's dense, beautiful prose and I did find precious things there, ripe and rampant, some hidden in lush foliage and others in open, blatant blooms. I let myself go, floating among the short stories, through the short novels, and, inevitably, taking that tawdry trip with Lo-lee-ta. When I got to Ada I began to feel tousled and full, poetry and allusion layering me like a cake—I had to set Ada aside and I confess that I have yet to finish it. I do return to the stories though, especially the illusory "That in Aleppo Once," a fretful, funny, and inscrutable short story. Though it has less to do with the now-tragic Syrian city than with the forever-tragic Othello, from which the title is derived, it inspired in me, nevertheless, a lifelong desire to travel to Aleppo. Now, I fear, it is too late, and I am contenting myself with the books I love and batches of muhammara, a suave mixture of roasted red pepper, nuts, bread, and garlic, all mashed together with olive oil and sweetened with a spoonful of pomegranate molasses. I scoop it up with bread or raw vegetables and hope for more peaceful days to come.

Makes 2 cups

2 large red bell peppers, roasted and peeled (see page 88)

½ teaspoon kosher or sea salt

½ cup fresh bread crumbs

½ cup almonds, toasted and, optionally, peeled (see page 15)

1 almond-size garlic clove, pounded (see page 6)

2 teaspoons cumin seeds, toasted (see page 14) and ground

Crushed red pepper flakes to taste

1 teaspoon red wine vinegar

1 tablespoon pomegranate molasses

¼ cup good olive oil, plus a little for pouring over

Combine all the ingredients in a blender or food processor and grind until smooth. Taste, adjust, and spread into a shallow bowl. Drizzle with olive oil and serve with bread—pitas are nice—or toasts.

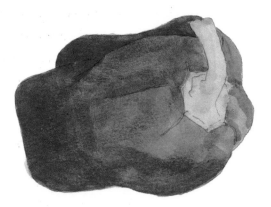

BAKED STUFFED VEGETABLES WITH ALMONDS, CURRANTS, SAFFRON, AND BREAD CRUMBS

My grandmother outlived my grandfather by more than twenty years. He was a radio man—a medium I very much appreciate myself—and smoked more cigars than could be considered healthy, an appreciation that I, thankfully, did not inherit. He was also quite tall, like me, and both of us loved my grandmother very much. Nana was always smart and vital, a good cook and voracious reader, but as she got older and moved into an assisted living apartment building, I worried that she might be lonely. I thought of her doing her crossword puzzles and looking out while Milwaukee carried on down below, the people and cars and boats on the river all so remote. Her studio apartment had an intercom to the residence office where they could help her if she needed something, and a panic button in the shower in case of emergency, but those were no good for loneliness. I wished that I lived closer to her and visited more so she could pretend to need help with the crossword and I could cook her dinner.

I know that I didn't invent comfort cooking, but I believe in it so strongly that I almost feel as if I did. Perhaps every evangelist has the sense that they are uniquely moved by their belief, so personally devoted to it, that it must be of them. I knew that I couldn't cook away the loneliness that had set in when Nana's husband died, but I thought I might be able to put it into remission for a bit, so I planned a visit. I told her I was going to make her some supper. She should invite her friends.

My mother called me the week before I was heading out there, very pleased that I was going. But she told me that the dinner party I was planning was making Nana nervous.

"I've already got the menu planned! Why is she nervous? She's gonna love it."

"I don't know. She thinks it's too much trouble and mess."

"I'll clean up! This is happening," I said, a little worked up and pounding the pulpit. "This is happening, Mom. It's going to be great and once it gets going, she'll relax."

Comfort by force, I thought, hanging up and checking that I had the ingredients that might be difficult to pick up in Milwaukee: saffron, pine nuts, and currants for the Sicilian classic pasta alla palina I planned to make. I was even checking a bag with a couple of my good knives and a bottle of decent olive oil.

"We can't do it here," Nana told me right off, after we'd hugged and said hello. "The kitchen in the common room is better. Mine is too small."

"Great!" I said, though I actually liked her cozy kitchen. I was glad that she wasn't trying to bail on the dinner altogether. It was scheduled for the next day, so we had some time to look through her old photographs and talk about the grandkids. She made tea and worked a crossword.

"Twenty-seven across," she said, "'Child of French cooking.' You ought to know that one."

"Julia," I said, though I knew that she knew. Pretty easy, must have been the local paper.

Next day, the cooking and dinner were a big success, though my mom was right: Nana was nervous.

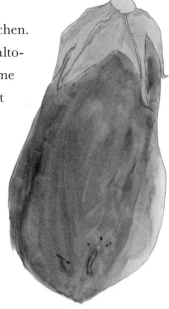

Nervous about the smell of the roasting cauliflower bothering people, about the big pot of water I was using for the pasta and how much salt I threw into it. She felt bad that I had to keep running back to her apartment for things and she worried about the mess I was making. I told her that it would all be cleaned up, that everyone would love it. I poured her a glass of wine, but my reassurances, and the tiny sip she took, weren't enough to smooth her edges. What finally calmed her down was one of her friends—and my new best friend—poking her head in to smile and say how delicious it smelled.

"And who is this handsome chef?" she exclaimed. Now I was in love. Nana beamed. She took a bigger sip of wine.

"Let's set the table," she said, taking her friend's arm. "Did you know he's come all the way from California? He wanted to make me dinner! A recipe from Sicily, he says."

After dinner, she looked tired and was starting to fret again, so I suggested she go to bed and leave the cleanup to me. Washing the dishes, I wondered about Nana's unease and if my cooking for her really was a comfort. I'd meant to relieve her loneliness, but suspected that, in a way, she didn't want relief. Maybe, I thought as I dried and put away the last of the plates and took the big pasta pot back to the neighbor we'd borrowed it from, the kind of loneliness that is specific to one person, heartache that has a direct object can be its own kind of comfort. Nana knew it, and she worked at not letting the cocoon of it enclose her, but it was hard. She was proud of me and she was glad that I came and cooked for her. But then dinner was over. It was time for bed and dreams of the one who can offer the truest comfort.

This recipe is another beauty from Sicily that has some of the same magic. It smells great, won't bother loved ones or anyone, and if things get messy, well, the better to remember them by.

3 tablespoons olive oil

1 small yellow onion, diced small

Kosher or sea salt

½ teaspoon saffron threads (about 10 threads), dried in a warm place and crushed to powder

1 teaspoon fennel seeds, toasted (see page 14) and ground

1 almond-size garlic clove, chopped

Crushed red pepper flakes

2 cups Toasted Bread Crumbs (page 50)

3 tablespoons almonds, toasted (see page 14)

2 tablespoons currants or raisins, plumped in hot water for 20 minutes, drained

1 teaspoon finely chopped marjoram or oregano leaves

2 tablespoons chopped parsley

¼ cup grated Parmesan or Pecorino Toscano

2 tablespoons good olive oil

18 pieces vegetables to stuff: artichokes, onions, zucchini, peppers, eggplant, tomatoes, fennel, leeks, cabbage leaves, kale leaves, or chard leaves (see page 37)

¼ cup dry white wine or water

Cooking oil, olive or vegetable

Heat a skillet to high and add the oil, then the onion and ¼ teaspoon salt. Stir until it gets going, then lower the heat and add the saffron and fennel seeds. Cook over low heat, adding a splash of water from time to time if needed, until soft but not browned, about 15 minutes. Move the onion to make a bare spot in the center of the skillet and add a little oil if needed, then the garlic and red pepper flakes. Cook until the garlic smells good but isn't yet brown, bring in the onion, stir, and turn out into a medium bowl to cool.

Heat the oven to 450°F.

Add the bread crumbs, almonds, currants or raisins, chopped herbs, Parmesan, and olive oil to the bowl with the cooked onion. Stir well, taste, and adjust.

Whatever vegetable you are going to stuff and bake, it has to be cooked first. The vegetables will cook more as they bake, but to ensure that you don't get an unpleasant bit of raw eggplant or artichoke, say, it is best to cook them at least partway before stuffing.

* *Tomatoes are the exception and can be halved, insides scooped out, and stuffed and baked, uncovered, from raw.*
* *Artichokes can be trimmed, choked, and boiled in salted water until tender, then stuffed either whole and upright or halved and on their sides.*
* *Onions can be halved, inner layers removed, seasoned, oiled, and baked, covered, until tender.*
* *Zucchini, peppers, and small to medium varieties of eggplant can be halved, insides scooped out, seasoned, oiled, and baked, covered, until tender.*
* *Fennel and large leeks can be trimmed, halved lengthwise, and boiled in salted water until tender, layers separated and stuffed or rolled around stuffing like fat cigars.*
* *Cabbage, kale, or chard leaves can be trimmed, boiled in salted water until tender, and rolled around stuffing like fat cigars.*

Arrange the stuffed vegetables in a baking dish that fits them snugly, pour the wine or water in the bottom of the dish, and drizzle with oil. Bake uncovered until the stuffing is heated through and browned on top, 15 to 20 minutes. Serve hot, warm, or at room temperature.

STEAMED CLAMS WITH ALMOND AND PARSLEY BUTTER AND NO LINGUINE

Sometimes, mid-cooking, I like to jettison my plan and make a new, better plan. The trick is knowing when it's better. I'm not saying I randomly hobble myself, cruelty-cooking-show style, it's just that it's exciting to change it up sometimes. And it surprises the family. Historically, some of the best jettison dinners at my house have started out as regular old pasta night and ended up as gather-around-the-skillet-with-bowls-and-bread night. This was one of those.

Makes 6 servings

¼ cup almonds, toasted (see page 14)

3 tablespoons unsalted butter, softened

½ cup loosely packed parsley leaves, finely chopped

2 tablespoons cooking oil, olive or vegetable

2 garlic cloves

Crushed red pepper flakes

3 pounds small clams, such as Manilas or Littlenecks, well washed in cold water

¼ cup dry white wine

A great loaf of rustic bread

Finely chop the almonds either by crushing with a rolling pin and chopping with a knife, or in a food processor. In a medium bowl, stir the almonds, butter, and parsley together until smooth. Don't add salt—the clams will do that. Set aside while you cook the clams.

Heat a large skillet to medium and add the oil, then the garlic and crushed red pepper flakes. Swirl the pan and, before the garlic browns at all, add the clams and wine. Cover the skillet and cook, stirring occasionally, until all the clams have opened. If a few won't open, that's okay; let them keep their deep secrets. Add the almond and parsley butter and stir so that it melts and mixes with the clam broth. Serve hot with spoons, bread, and napkins.

Variation: Do it the way I originally planned and pluck some, or all, of the cooked clams from their shells, return to the skillet, and toss with hot boiled linguine.

SWEET CORN WITH ALMONDS AND SAGE

My dad likes to tell a story about a field of corn he once grew on a low-lying wedge of land, between the pond and the big alfalfa field on our New Jersey farm. Too small for the usual hay crop, and with hard access under the big walnut branches, it was mostly fallow: milkweedy, with black-eyed Susans and Queen Anne's lace. In the summer the growth was lush and walking through difficult—waist high in green that grabbed and left wiry seedpods in our socks as we headed for frog and snake excursions in the swamp below the pond run-off.

In winter we could walk out onto the solid frozen swamp to the dead trees that my dad had marked for firewood. The crashed-down trunks we would cut into logs and drag with a tractor and chain up from the swamp to the edge of the field. The ice was usually thick enough to hold a tractor, but one time the tires broke through, just the front two, so that it stood with snout tilted down to the cold mud and frozen chunks. The exhaust stack blew blasts of gray smoke into the gray sky, and the tires made sloppy sounds as they rocked but got no release—the swamp had us and the big rear wheels just spun. When a second tractor strained in vain to extract the first, snapping a chain and sending a thick, lethal link whistling past my ear, we gave up. It started snowing as we walked home and that night there was a hard freeze, ice reforming around the hunched tractor, trapped like a mastodon.

That spring, we built a fire under the tractor's iron belly to melt the flood waters that had thawed and refrozen in its guts all winter. In the end it took a bulldozer—low treaded and thumping—to finally pull the smoking tractor out. Slack and broken, tires flopping and dark like live swamp things, it exhaled a gush of oily water, but it was not dead. On a warm day a month later, my dad pulled a plow behind the drained, dried, and rebuilt tractor and folded under the weeds, smoothed the soil, and planted sweet corn in that little field. When it was ready, we built another fire, this time under our biggest kitchen kettle: Dad said he wanted to taste corn as fresh as it can get, shucked and boiled right in the field. We ate a lot of hot ears that day and all through August—boys' shirtless fronts streaked with butter and pulp, girls fishing kernels out of their bathing suit tops. On the hottest nights, we'd wade and flop into the pond, bits of corn floating off us in slicks, shining on the bad-smelling water.

This recipe doesn't taste like my dad's corn—Silver Queen, I think it was. This one's more crunch and sage than pond and smoke, and that's a good thing. The sweetness, though—Dad gets credit for that.

Makes 6 side dish servings

4 tablespoons (½ stick) unsalted butter

1 medium yellow onion, diced small

Kosher or sea salt

Leaves from 4 sage sprigs (about 20 leaves), roughly chopped

4 or 5 ears corn, shucked and silk rubbed off with a kitchen towel

½ cup almonds, toasted (see page 14) and chopped

In a large skillet, melt 3 tablespoons of the butter over medium-high heat. Add the onion and ¼ teaspoon salt. Stir until it gets going, then lower the heat and cook, stirring occasionally and adding a splash of water from time to time if needed, until soft but not browned, about 15 minutes. Move the onion to the edges of the skillet, add the remaining tablespoon butter, and, when it melts, the sage. Stir the sizzling sage for 30 seconds, then add the corn, ½ teaspoon salt, and ½ cup water. Stir and bring to a simmer over high heat, then lower to just maintain the simmer and cook until the corn is tender, about 10 minutes. Stir in the almonds, taste, adjust, and eat with . . .

. . . grilled eggplants, peppers, or squashes . . . sliced tomatoes . . . poached eggs and a little something spicy . . . or fold leftovers into an omelet or stir into ricotta and bake.

PARSLEY AND WALNUT PESTO
WITH PECORINO TOSCANO

I have learned a serious and sad thing about pine nuts since I published a recipe for classic pesto in *Twelve Recipes*. Most pine nuts in the United States come from the cones of the Korean pine, collected in the forests of China and far eastern Russia. I love the idea of eating wild foods, but when they are harvested in great quantity, as these pine nuts are, there are inevitable attendant problems such as habitat destruction and over-harvesting. We are not the only ones who like sweet pine nuts: bears and boars fatten up on them, chipmunks and deer nibble them. Without supplies of pine nuts, Siberian tigers have fewer deer to stalk and bears get hungry and start wandering into towns in search of sustenance.

Non-Chinese pine nuts, from Italy or North America, are very expensive even if you manage to find them, so farmed almonds or walnuts are better, more affordable choices. There is a work-around if you miss the resinous flavor that pine nuts have generously given us all these years: mastic, the sun-dried sap harvested from cultivated *Pistacia lentiscus* trees. Most mastic comes from the Greek island of Chios—the beautiful amber droplets are sometimes known as "tears of Chios." Find them online or at Greek or Middle Eastern markets and grind them in with the garlic and walnuts.

I like the sweetness of aged Pecorino Toscano for this, but if what you have is Parmesan, that's good too.

Makes enough for 1 pound pasta

Leaves from 1 big bunch washed and dried parsley, about 3 cups, lightly packed

1 almond-size garlic clove, pounded (see page 6)

Scant ¼ teaspoon kosher or sea salt

¼ cup walnuts, toasted (see page 14) and pounded or finely ground

½ teaspoon mastic, ground to powder (optional)

½ cup grated Pecorino Toscano

½ cup olive oil

Push half of the parsley leaves down into a blender. Add the garlic, salt, walnuts, mastic (if using), and Pecorino, top with the remaining parsley leaves, and push it all down hard with a spoon. Add the olive oil and begin the pulse and push method. You don't want the blender to grind up only the leaves that are at the bottom, nor do you want it too finely pureed. The solution is to pulse the blender for a second, stir the contents with a spoon, and then tamp it all back down. Pulse again, push it down again. Repeat this process, taking care to remove the spoon before running the blender. Keep going until it catches, the sound changes, and it all spins. Let it go for several seconds. The pesto should have flow but not be entirely smooth. Taste and add what's needed, then pulse a final time to mix in any additions.

Pesto is good everywhere, especially when summer tomatoes are involved, but also:

* *over grilled vegetables*
* *stuffed in an omelet*
* *spread in a sandwich*
* *stirred into hot rice*
* *dolloped into bowls of soup*

DUKKAH

The classic way to eat dukkah is with soft bread dipped in good olive oil and then in a saucer of nutty, spicy dukkah. It can go lots of other places and I usually stand there at the counter, stuffing pinches of dukkah into my mouth while I'm dreaming of those exotic places. The sumac is a colorful, lemony, nontraditional addition.

Makes ¾ cup

1 tablespoon coriander seeds

2 teaspoons cumin seeds

¼ cup sesame seeds

½ cup almonds, toasted (see page 14)

2 teaspoons ground sumac

Marash, Urfa, Aleppo, or other dried and crushed mild red pepper to taste

Freshly ground black pepper

¼ teaspoon kosher or sea salt

Heat a small skillet to medium and add the coriander and cumin seeds. Shake the pan occasionally and toast until the seeds smell good and begin to wiggle in the skillet, about 30 seconds. Set the spices aside and toast the sesame seeds in the same skillet until they are lightly browned and starting to pop, about 1 minute. Set aside.

Crush the coriander and cumin seeds with a mortar and pestle until nearly powdered. Add the almonds and crush to medium fine—depending on the size of your mortar, you may need to do this in batches. Stir in the sesame seeds, sumac, Marash or other pepper, grindings of black pepper, and the salt. Eat a lot and keep what is left in a jar with a tight lid in the pantry.

Sprinkle big pinches of dukkah on:

* *Plain whole-milk yogurt (drained or not) or soft cheese, as a dip or just to eat*
* *Beans, lentils, or chickpeas, whole or pureed smooth*
* *Grilled eggplant and other vegetables, fish, or chicken*
* *Fennel or artichokes—cooked wedges or raw and very thinly sliced*
* *Eggs*
* *Sliced ripe tomatoes, cucumbers, melon, and roasted peppers*
* *Your ideas . . .*

GREENS GRATIN WITH CASHEWS, CILANTRO, GINGER, AND BREAD CRUMBS

I have a Greek-American friend who writes and directs very funny screenplays. He also loves to cook and wanted a lesson while I was visiting him in L.A. We started drinking wine and ran out of time to make the moussaka we'd been dreaming about, so we settled on just the béchamel instead—my friend said he was sure I was a bech king. And it's true, I do have a mania for béchamel sauce. I guess it's a royal obsession, but not carnal: A sauce made from buttoned-up cow's milk thickened with lily white wheat flour is more old friend than new lover. There's a little butter involved, sure, but nothing to pant about. Maybe for me it's the thrill of near scorching, the vigorous whisking while flirting with disaster. Probably it has more to do with comfort and versatility: a smooth, substantial sauce that is as staid as it is willing.

Still, not every gratin wants béchamel, and after several versions of this one, I found out I preferred simple cream instead. The cilantro and ginger provide aromatics, the cashews and crumbs some heft, and the cream gives nice flow.

Makes 6 servings

3 tablespoons cooking oil, olive or vegetable

1 medium yellow onion, diced

Kosher or sea salt

2 teaspoons minced ginger

1 to 2 almond-size garlic cloves, chopped

1 overflowing cup roughly chopped cilantro stems and leaves (about ½ bunch)

Crushed red pepper flakes

2 bunches lacinato or other kale, leaves stripped from stems, roughly chopped or torn, washed, drained but not dried

1 cup cream

½ cup cashews, toasted (see page 14) and finely chopped or crushed

2 cups Toasted Bread Crumbs (recipe follows)

Heat the oven to 425°F.

Heat a skillet over high heat and add the oil, then the onion and ½ teaspoon salt. Stir until it gets going, then turn to low and cook, stirring occasionally, until soft and very lightly browned, 15 to 20 minutes. Use a lid or a splash of water if coloring too much before getting soft. Add the ginger, garlic, cilantro, and red pepper flakes and stir while they sizzle for 30 seconds or so. Add the kale and a pinch of salt and raise the heat to high. Stir occasionally as the kale wilts, then turn the heat to low and cover. Cook, stirring occasionally and adding water if it starts to sizzle, until the kale is tender, about 15 minutes. Taste a piece to be sure, then add the cream and cashews. Stir while it comes back to a simmer over high heat. There should be a good amount of liquid around the kale—much will evaporate while the gratin bakes. Add a ladleful of water if it seems at all thick at this point.

Turn the greens out into a baking dish, or just leave in the skillet, top with the bread crumbs, and bake until bubbling in the middle and nicely browned on top, 8 to 10 minutes.

TOASTED BREAD CRUMBS

Makes 4 cups

With a serrated knife, carve the crust off a 1-pound loaf of good rustic bread and tear it into 1½-inch pieces. Grind coarsely in a food processor or blender, then toss in a bowl with ¼ cup olive oil and ½ teaspoon kosher or sea salt. The crumbs should be tasty and pretty oily, though not totally soaked. Spread onto a baking sheet and bake at 350°F for 7 minutes (I use a timer). With a metal spatula, scoop the crumbs into a pile, stir them around a bit, and spread them back out. Back into the oven for 5 minutes and repeat with the spatula. Keep baking and stirring, resetting the timer each time, until the crumbs are done: if they are to be sprinkled onto plates of food and not baked further, they should be the color of brown sugar and very crisp; if using to top a dish that's going back in the oven to finish, the crumbs should be more like light brown sugar and still a bit soft.

Keep unused crumbs in a jar with a tight lid in the refrigerator. Re-crisp in a hot oven for a few minutes before using.

CELERY AND APPLE SALAD WITH POUNDED ALMONDS, ANCHOVIES, PARMESAN, AND PARSLEY

Common celery can achieve an emerald, swoosh-shaped chic when thinly bias-sliced and creatively dressed. Together, Parmesan, anchovies, and almonds could create a force so savory as to lay a softer salad low, but crisp-sweet apple and juicy-fresh celery welcome such a show of strength. A big handful of hearty escarole, frisée, or curly endive provides structure, and tender parsley leaves give green aromatics. The first time I made it, I bragged that I'd given celery an upgrade from salad bar shabby to Rainbow Room chic.

"Maybe," one friend said, bread-mopping her plate, "or maybe it's just weird, anchovies and apples," she went on, reaching for the platter. "Can I have some more?"

Makes 4 to 6 servings

Kosher or sea salt

6 celery stalks, trimmed, washed, and thinly sliced at a long angle

2 tablespoons almonds, toasted (see page 14)

1 almond-size garlic clove

4 anchovy fillets

Freshly ground black pepper

Juice of ½ lemon

1 teaspoon cider vinegar

3 tablespoons good olive oil

2 crisp apples, such as Gala or Pink Lady

1 medium head frisée, green leaf-tips trimmed away and core removed so that leaves are loose

½ cup parsley leaves, whole if tender, or roughly chopped

Parmesan

Bring a pot of water to a boil for the celery. Add salt till it tastes right, then add the celery and boil till tender, about 5 minutes. It should be nearly soft with a little crispness still—taste pieces occasionally to know when it's there. Drain and spread on a platter to cool.

Meanwhile, make the dressing: Roughly crush the almonds with a mortar and pestle. Set the almonds aside and pound the garlic with a pinch of salt in the mortar until nearly liquid. Add the anchovies and pound to a paste. Add half of the almonds back in and pound to a paste again. Grind in some black pepper and stir in the lemon juice, vinegar, and ¼ teaspoon salt. Stir in the olive oil, taste, correct, and set aside.

Cut a thin slice from one of the apples and taste to see what the skin is like. If it seems tough, peel the apples, then quarter, core, and thinly slice them. In a salad bowl, combine the apple, celery, frisée, and parsley and toss with most of the dressing and a pinch of salt. Taste, adjust, and arrange on a platter. Drizzle the remaining dressing on top and sprinkle with the remaining almonds and slivers or gratings of Parmesan.

PORK MEATBALLS WITH FARRO, HAZELNUTS, AND SAGE

A combination of hamburgers and humiliation made me include this recipe. A friend asked me to help with a better burger project he was working on, aiming to replace a third of the meat with more sustainable, but no less delicious, ingredients. Sometimes denigrated as filler, I think of additions of things like bread or rice, vegetables or mushrooms, as contributing flavor and tenderness to ground meats. I was in, I told him, but I'm not really a hamburger guy—I eat about two a year, one, guiltily, at a highway In-N-Out, and the other, gloriously, at someplace great, like KronnerBurger in Oakland.

Meatballs, on the other hand, I love all the time, and they bring me to the humiliation part. I thought I made good meatballs until my friend pointed out that his were better. He said it in a semi-nice way, saying it was the *one thing* he made better than me. After a delicious but debilitating comparison, I saw that he was right and, eyes opened, I noticed that the upstairs chefs at Chez Panisse were besting me, too. My ball game needed upping. I got rolling, and I'm not saying mine are better than anyone's, but they've definitely gotten better.

I probably wouldn't, but if I were going to make this recipe into hamburgers Italiano-style, I'd grill them and melt on some cheese, maybe mozzarella or even a sweet Gorgonzola, skip the ketchup, and pile on some crunchy lettuce.

Kosher or sea salt

Scant ½ cup farro

1 pound ground pork

¼ cup cooking oil, olive or vegetable

1 medium yellow onion, diced small

Leaves from 4 sage sprigs (about 20 leaves), roughly chopped

2 almond-size garlic cloves, finely chopped

Crushed red pepper flakes to taste

1 egg

1 tablespoon cream, half-and-half, or milk

1 cup fresh bread crumbs

Loose ½ cup grated Parmesan

⅓ cup finely (more or less) chopped hazelnuts

Bring 2 quarts of water to a boil and add salt till it tastes right (see page 8). Rinse the farro and add it to the pot, stirring once or twice. Lower the heat so it keeps bubbling but doesn't foam over, and cook until tender, about 20 minutes, but taste to be sure. Drain and spread on a plate to cool.

Spread the pork out on a platter or tray and season with ½ teaspoon salt. Mix the salt in briefly—over-kneading ground meats makes them tougher. Set aside.

Meanwhile, heat a skillet to medium-high and add the oil, onion, and a sprinkle of salt. Stir until it gets going, then turn the heat to medium-low. Cover loosely and stir from time to time, adding a splash of water if needed, until the onion is soft but not browned, about 15 minutes. Add the sage, garlic, and the crushed red pepper flakes. Stir until it smells very good, 30 seconds or so, and turn out onto a plate to cool.

In a mixing bowl large enough to hold all the ingredients, whisk together the egg and cream or milk. Stir in the bread crumbs and leave them to soak up the liquid for 5 minutes. Add the pork, farro, onion-garlic-sage, Parmesan, and hazelnuts and mix very well, squeezing the mixture through your fingers.

Decide how you're going to cook the meatballs: frying them in a skillet is messiest and arguably best; flattening them slightly and grilling is least messy and very good; roasting them on a baking sheet in a very hot oven is easy and lovely. Heat up whichever device you're going to use and cook a mini patty for a taster and correct the mixture as needed for salt, spice, cheese, and so on. Using your hands, roll meatballs about the size of Ping-Pong balls. Cook and eat in appropriate meatball ways: in tomato-y sauce with pasta, on a roll, with garlicky yogurt . . . or, make them tinier and eat out of hand with drinks.

CAULIFLOWER WITH ALMOND AILLADE

Aillade is like aïoli without the egg. Hey, it's vegan! Thing is, its egglessness leaves it with a slightly weaker constitution (like some undernourished vegans I know), and so it can break more easily. Happily, it doesn't matter if it breaks—carry on and it will all come together when it hits the hot cauliflower and a little water. Untoasted almonds let their sweetness show, and quickly boiling and peeling them gives aillade that almost mayonnaise-like look.

Makes about 1 cup

1 almond-size garlic clove (or more)

Kosher or sea salt

¼ cup peeled raw almonds (see page 15)

¾ cup good olive oil

1 teaspoon lemon juice or vinegar (white wine, Champagne, or cider)

2 tablespoons finely chopped parsley

Freshly ground black pepper

1 large cauliflower head (about 2 pounds) cut into Ping-Pong-ball-size florets

Put a large pot of water on to boil for the cauliflower while you make the aillade.

Pound the garlic in a mortar and pestle with a pinch of salt, add the almonds and pound to a chunky paste, not entirely smooth. Stir in 1 tablespoon of water and

then begin adding olive oil in a thin stream, like making mayonnaise. When half the oil is in, add another tablespoon of water if it's getting very thick, then keep stirring in the remaining oil. Add the lemon juice or vinegar, chopped parsley, black pepper, and a pinch of salt. Taste and adjust with more lemon or salt and add a splash of water if it needs more flow.

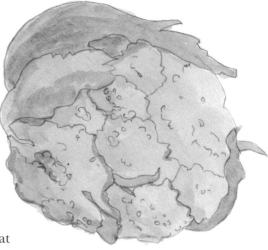

Add salt to the pot of boiling water and taste that it's right (see page 8). Add the cauliflower and cook until tender—about 5 minutes, but tasting a piece is the only way to really know. Stir a couple of tablespoons of the cooking water into the bowl of aillade to get it in the mood. Set aside a little more cooking water for possible adjustments, then drain the cauliflower and put it in a mixing bowl. Stir in the aillade. Taste and adjust for flavor with salt or lemon, and for texture with a splash of cooking water or oil.

* *Smash up a few anchovy fillets with the garlic and almonds.*
* *Aillade is also a good dressing for boiled green beans, fennel, or asparagus, or spooned over grilled vegetables, fish, or chicken.*

ALMOND GRANITA

There was no beach.

Even in the morning, August in Portopalo di Capo Passero at the southern tip of Sicily was sun-blasted hot and so bright it was colorless. We stepped down from the bus, gasping like fish gone aground as it pulled away and looking through the dust for the shop where we'd get the key, learn how to turn the water on, and, if we were lucky, get a ride.

"*Sì, ma non c'è una spiaggia,*" the shopkeeper said, shaking her head when we asked if we could please have the key to the English signora's beach house. "Yes, but there is no beach."

We were stricken. We loved the beach, we loved the word for beach: *spiaggia*. We came here for the beach!

I was speechless, but Kathleen, intrepid, asked, "But there is the sea, yes?"

"*Sì,*" she said, gesturing broadly to indicate Sicily, the *island* we were on, "*c'è siempre il mare!*" There is always the sea.

It was a hot half hour walk to the house, she told us, but we could get a ride with her son if we wanted to wait an hour. We accepted, knowing that an hour could, in fact, mean any number of hours, and headed to the café. It was too hot for coffee and too early (if there is such a thing) for Prosecco, so we ordered what everyone else was having: flaky brioche rolls to dip into icy almond granita, Sicilian breakfast. After a couple of hours and still no ride, it was definitely no longer too early for Prosecco.

The house, it turned out, was on a volcanic rocky stretch of coast, and we loved it. The sea was blue and cold and we waded in, harvesting sea urchin from the rocks and slurping down their salty roes with more Prosecco. There were greenhouses in the fields nearby—long rows of frames flapping with tattered, end-of-season strips of plastic sheeting. The harvest was done and we'd been instructed to take all we wanted of the small plum-shaped tomatoes that were left on the vines. Sweet and seemingly pre-seasoned by hard-scrabble soil and salty sea spray, we ate little else.

Whenever I am burning for tomatoes or urchin to match those of Portopalo di Capo Passero, this almond granita cools me down.

Makes 1+ quart

2 cups whole milk	8 ounces almond paste
½ cup sugar	⅛ teaspoon kosher or sea salt

Combine all the ingredients with 2 cups water in a blender and puree until smooth. Freeze in an ice cream maker according to the manufacturer's instructions. If you don't eat it all now, put it, covered, in the freezer for later, but make sure to temper it in the refrigerator for 30 to 45 minutes before scooping.

TOTALLY BAKED PEACH

An Oakland chef I know hates reggae, the Beatles, pizza, and pot—local favorites all, but he's from L.A. and is more punk, pills, paella, and the waves at El Porto. Just to mess with him I served him this dessert, squinting and drawling, "It's a totally baked peach. Stoned." It wasn't, of course, dosed, but I didn't lie: The stone *had* been taken out, replaced with a buttery, nutty nugget, and baked. *Totally.*

Though my chef friend has a dim view of weed, his home city, and many cities, seems to feel differently: There are some sophisticated concoctions being cooked up and a fun and funny TV show that features chefs, a chocolatier, a cannabis specialist, and a happy happy host. I guess I fall somewhere in between. For me, medicated edibles are like good wines: I don't make them myself, but I might try a sip.

Makes 6 servings

¼ cup almonds, toasted (see page 14)

¼ cup walnuts, toasted (see page 14)

½ cup plus 2 tablespoons all-purpose flour

¼ cup lightly packed brown sugar

¼ teaspoon kosher or sea salt

5 tablespoons cool unsalted butter

3 large, freestone peaches

Granulated sugar

Crème fraiche, vanilla ice cream, or cream (whipped or not), for serving

Finely chop the almonds and walnuts and mix in a medium bowl with the flour, sugar, and salt. Cut the butter into little cubes and crush them into the nut mixture, using your fingers but not your whole hot hand, until there are no big butter lumps and the mixture is still crumbly but holds together moistly when squeezed. Set the topping aside.

Heat the oven to 425°F.

Cut the peaches in half through the stem ends and twist the halves apart. Remove the stones and cut a little sliver to taste and get a sense of how much granulated sugar to sprinkle over the peaches. Set the halves cut side up in a baking dish and sprinkle with the appropriate amount of sugar—somewhere between none and 1 tablespoon. Squeeze a small handful of the topping into an egg shape and fit into the pit divot. Repeat with the remaining peach halves, add water to the dish to just cover the bottom, and bake uncovered until the peaches are tender, about 30 to 40 minutes. Serve hot or warm with crème fraîche, vanilla ice cream, or cream.

ALMOND BUTTER COOKIES WITH CHOCOLATE

I read about a Girl Scout who sold 16,000 boxes of those famous cookies by describing "a bleak, flavorless wasteland . . . as flavorless as dirt. I give it a 1." She's right (other than frozen Thin Mints). As a guy who is not a cute Girl Scout master of the undersell, I think I'll try a different approach: These are the *best* peanut butter cookies, but even better because they're *almond* butter cookies. Nostalgically scouty, but crisp and chewy with dark chocolate chunks that combine with the almond's warm toastiness to make them a singular joy! A 10!

Makes about 30 cookies

8 tablespoons (1 stick) unsalted butter, at soft room temperature

½ cup granulated sugar, plus a little for rolling

½ cup lightly packed brown sugar

½ cup crunchy or smooth almond butter

1 egg

1 teaspoon pure vanilla extract

1½ cups all-purpose flour

½ teaspoon kosher or sea salt

1 teaspoon baking soda

¼ cup almonds, toasted (see page 14) and crushed or chopped

4 ounces dark chocolate, chopped (or dark chocolate chips)

Heat the oven to 325°F.

In a large bowl, cream the butter with a wooden spoon until it is pale and light. Add the sugars and beat until smooth. Stir in the almond butter, egg, and vanilla extract until completely mixed. Sift in the flour, salt, and baking soda and stir until a smooth dough forms. Stir in the almonds and chocolate. Tell the kids not to eat any of the dough. Turn your back and secretly eat some of the dough. Pretend not to notice the kids eating the dough.

Roll the remaining dough, if any, into Ping-Pong-size balls and roll each lightly in granulated sugar. Place the balls on a baking sheet, 2 inches apart, and crisscross-fork them flat (use 2 sheets if you're baking the whole batch—see note). Bake until golden brown, 10 to 12 minutes.

Note: I usually bake just the cookies we are going to eat today and freeze the rest to bake fresh, as cravings arise. Place the leftover dough on a piece of plastic wrap. With damp hands so it doesn't stick, form the dough into a log, wrap tightly, and freeze. Cut pieces to sugar, flatten, and bake when you're ready.

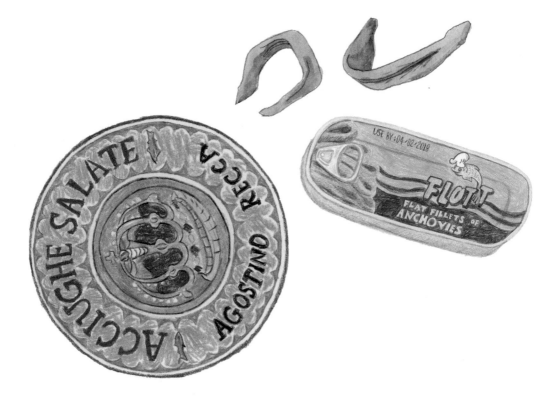

anchovies

I like to think that because you are even reading this book, and the anchovy section in particular, you are already an anchoviphile drooling for new recipes. However, if you arrived anchovy-curious, or if you think you are a hater, rolling in it for the revulsion, I am here nevertheless, ready and proud to be your guide, savior, and pusherman.

First, forget about the fishy brown bits that appeared on the "everything" pizza you ordered that time, ruining the party. That's not what we are talking about here. Maybe you're thinking right now about some things you picked off a Niçoise salad and wondering if *those* were anchovies? *Oh no, I certainly don't like those!* Maybe you even tried cooking with them yourself, having heard the hype, but it didn't work out and the rest of the jar is still in the fridge? Go throw that out right now, because the truth

is that no matter what the quality of the anchovies you buy, they are at their best when first opened, and then good for only a couple of days.

But enough about the worst. The best anchovies, whether salt- or oil-packed, open up a world of flavor that is surely of the ocean, but with a salty, solidly ashore savor that can be as un-ignorable as it is unde-tectable and as chewy as a sip of seawater. You'll know it when you taste it in a good Caesar salad, in spaghetti alla puttanesca, or in warm, buttery bagna cauda.

Anchovies are available several ways. The pickled type, boquerones, are delicious to have as they are, with drinks, but I don't really cook with them. Salted anchovies are what I use, and they come two ways: whole, headless, and packed in salt; and fillets packed in oil. Both are good and deciding which to cook with is mostly about how many anchovies you are going to use and how much time you have. Salt-packed anchovies, which often come in larger cans, need filleting before use—it's not hard and only mildly graphic. To do it, rinse the salt off the number of anchovies that you plan to use now and put them in a bowl of cold water to soak for 10 minutes. Cover any anchovies remaining in the can with a layer of salt to keep in the fridge for later. Lift an an-chovy out of the bowl of water and, with your fingers, open the abdominal cavity to find

the spine. Starting at the head end, pull one of the fillets away from the spine, swish it in the water, and set aside, then repeat with the other fillet. It's okay if they tear a little, but if the fillets are stiff and sticking to the spine, let them soak a few minutes more to soften. Discard the bones, bits, and water and drip a little oil onto the fillets, especially if you're not using them right away.

Oil-packed fillets are easier and often just as good. They generally come in 2-ounce cans that contain 10 to 12 fillets. If you don't use the whole can in your recipe, either snack on the rest (I recommend on buttered bread with a cold glass of pink or white) or leave unused fillets in their oil and refrigerate for up to 2 days.

CUCUMBER AND GREEN TOMATO SALAD WITH AVOCADO, FISH SAUCE, CILANTRO, AND LIME

Sometimes the idea that you thought was best, your favorite idea, is the one that's gotta go. It took many years of creating daily menus at Chez Panisse for me to realize, and then fully accept, this hard reality: That dish that felt so perfect rolling around on the tongue of my mind's mouth—it rarely made the final cut. I'd end up editing it when the rest of the menu failed to fall into place around it, or when I caught some of the WTF glances among the cooks at the menu meeting. It's okay, I told myself, back at the cutting board, you can always save Precious for later, and rethinking your starting point can get you to a different, better finish line.

There's a salad that got bumped around my back burners for a while: porcini mushrooms and green tomatoes, both raw and very thinly sliced, with garlic vinaigrette, mint, and Parmesan shavings. Simple and elegant, it is doable only at that moment in spring when green tomatoes and fresh, firm, snow-melt porcini coincide. I knew it was good, had made it at home many times, and when it eventually made it past the censor and onto the restaurant menu, it won many new admirers and the tart, clean crunch of its raw green tomatoes inspired further improvisations. Try this, one of mine, and start composing your own.

Makes 6 servings

1 almond-size garlic clove, pounded (see page 6)

Kosher or sea salt

Juice of half a lime

1 teaspoon rice vinegar or white wine vinegar

½ teaspoon fish sauce (or more to taste; I like Red Boat brand for its flavor and lots of other brands for their cool labels)

Freshly ground black pepper

Diced jalapeño or other hot pepper, to taste

1 shallot, finely diced, or 3 or 4 scallions, all the white and most of the green parts, thinly sliced

¼ cup good olive oil

2 baseball-size green, unripe tomatoes (about 1 pound), cored

1 cucumber, peeled

6 cilantro sprigs, roughly chopped

1 large ripe avocado

Make the dressing: In a small mixing bowl, stir together the pounded garlic, ¼ teaspoon salt, the lime juice, vinegar, and fish sauce, and grind in some black pepper. Stir in the jalapeño and shallot or scallions, let sit for 10 minutes, then stir in the olive oil and set aside.

Slice the green tomatoes as thinly as possible and spread them out on a platter. Sprinkle with salt, being sure to get all the slices. Thinly slice the cucumber and toss in a mixing bowl with a pinch of salt, the cilantro, and half the dressing. Taste, adjust, and spread the cucumbers over the tomatoes. Top the salad with scoops or slices of avocado, sprinkle them with salt, and then spoon the remaining dressing on top.

Variation: Very thinly slice firm fresh porcini or button mushrooms instead of the cucumbers. Use a lemon-garlic dressing, chopped parsley, and mint. Thinly slice the green tomatoes, spread them on a platter, then spread the mushrooms. Drizzle with good olive oil, skip the avocado, and sprinkle with Parmesan shavings. Like a little stroll from forest to vine to dairy to garden.

ARTICHOKES AND NEW ONIONS BAKED WITH ANCHOVIES AND BREAD CRUMBS

Kathleen and I have been married for thirty years. Happy is too simple a word for it, it's more than that. Happiness is like when I was a kid and got a bright beautiful balloon, the one I really wanted, and it's full, not of air, but of some magical stuff that lifts it up, and makes it fly and makes me smile when it comes back because I've got a hold of it. Maybe happy *is* the right word.

We've done a lot together, but one thing Kathleen and I don't really do is cook together. We do, a little; she spins the lettuce after it's washed and talks to me while I make vinagrette and she trims the green beans. If it's someone's birthday, she bakes a cake. Okay, we cook together. But when I am with a friend like Russell Moore—the kind of brilliant restaurant chef who also knows from good home-cooking—we're not just divvying up tasks, we're collaborating, really *cooking*. It feels satisfying, like in a restaurant kitchen when the team's humming, but more intimate and fun: The pressure's off, wine's been poured, we're cooking for ourselves, and it will be just the way we like it, no complaints, no crybabies (other than actual babies).

This is a recipe that Russ and I cooked together at Chez Panisse, where, especially when I was cooking with my good friend, it felt like home. Russ thought we should make a gratin with artichokes and sweet new spring onions, but in little bundles instead of spread out flat. We roasted the onions first, then curled them around the boiled artichoke hearts, tucked in anchovies, sprinkled bread crumbs. We served them with grilled, sliced lamb and spoonfuls of salsa verde, but they would be just as good with eggs and a green salad. And salsa verde, and a friend.

Makes 6 servings

1 lemon

6 medium artichokes

Kosher or sea salt

1 tablespoon good olive oil, plus more to drizzle

1 tablespoon white or red wine vinegar

1 bay leaf

1 garlic clove, cracked but unpeeled

½ cup dry white wine (optional)

2 thyme sprigs, leaves picked from stems and finely chopped (optional)

6 new onions or 12 large scallions

One 2-ounce can anchovy fillets (10 to 12 fillets), draned and halved lengthwise

1 cup Toasted Bread Crumbs (page 50)

Heat the oven to 450°F.

Squeeze half the lemon into a bowl of cold water big enough to hold the artichokes. Snap the leaves off the artichokes until the lower third is yellow or very pale green. Cut off the green top parts of the leaves and any of the stem that's too tough, then peel the base and stem with a paring knife or a vegetable peeler. Cut in half lengthwise and, with a spoon, scoop out and discard the hairy choke, if any, and drop the artichokes into the lemon water to prevent discoloring. When all the artichokes are trimmed, discard the lemon water and put the artichoke halves into a large saucepan. Sprinkle with 1 teaspoon salt and let them sit to absorb it for a few minutes. Add the olive oil, vinegar, bay leaf, garlic,

¼ cup wine, and thyme, if using. Add another teaspoon salt and just enough cold water to barely cover the artichokes, then bring to a boil over high heat. Lower the heat to a slow simmer and taste the water for salt, adding more if needed. Cook until tender, about 10 minutes. A paring knife should meet very little resistance when inserted into the heart of an artichoke. Drain and set aside to cool.

Trim the root hairs and most of the green tops from the new onions and cut them in half lengthwise (if using scallions, leave all the green tops on and just trim the root end). Rinse to remove any dirt, then spread the onions on a baking sheet, drizzle with oil, and sprinkle with salt. Roll the onions around to distribute the oil and salt, spread them out, and bake until tender, about 15 minutes. Sprinkle with a little water if they are getting too browned but are not yet done. Lower the oven to 350°F.

In a large casserole or skillet, curl the onion halves around the artichoke halves to make little bundles. Tuck 2 anchovy fillets into each bundle, sprinkle generously with the bread crumbs, and drizzle with oil. Pour the remaining wine or water into the casserole or skillet and bake until hot and nicely browned, about 15 minutes. Squeeze the other lemon half over just before serving.

CELERY AND RADISHES WITH ANCHOVY BUTTER

One of the pleasures/perils of a life in the restaurant business is good wine, and over the years/glasses I have made friends with some very fine people making delicious, generous wines. In some cases, the generosity extends to providing a nice quiet place for a chef to write: At Hudson Vineyards in Napa and their neighbor just across the Sonoma county line, Scribe Winery, the muses and rosés have done their parts to get my cookbooks written.

One night, out of focus, out of words, and distracted by the plaintive coyote cry-laughing beneath my window, I closed my laptop and headed into the town of Sonoma for a late supper. I brought along my reading glasses and Raymond Chandler, since I don't mind being that loner nerding out with a book at the bar. I ordered the radishes with anchovy butter and a bacon, lettuce, and fried green tomato sandwich, and they were very tasty, but the bartender's conversation kept me from my book. Recounting the loss of over a third of his flock of sheep to predators (in Sonoma, apparently, the bartenders are also shepherds), he said that eight of his lambs had been killed in a single night that spring.

"Only one of them really eaten,"

he remembered sadly as I tore like a carnivore into my sandwich, bacon snapping and hot tomato juice spattering, "the rest just killed. For the sport, I guess."

I started eating too quickly, scooping up anchovy butter on a second radish as I was still crunching through the first. Predator talk was making me nervous, thinking about that coyote under my window, wondering how many pack-mates he had and if I might have mistaken plaintive for desperately hungry. Maybe I was steeling myself for a canine encounter, eating fast and furious to preemptively alpha dog the pack and make it back to my room unbitten. I realize radishes and a fancy sandwich are far too twee to impress born killers, but that's what I had. I cruelly ripped the leaves from a breakfast radish, not caring where the Himalayan pink salt flew! I growled, practicing. Not, I hope, out loud.

Dipping clean, crisp radishes and celery in pungent, smooth anchovy butter does not deter varmints, but goes well with glasses of cold rosé, so do it anyway.

Makes 6 servings

1 bunch radishes

6 celery stalks

1 almond-size garlic clove

One 2-ounce can anchovy fillets (10 to 12 fillets), drained

4 tablespoons (½ stick) unsalted butter, at room temperature

Kosher or sea salt

Trim the radishes and celery as needed and give them a wash. Set aside to drain, in the fridge if you like.

Pound the garlic and anchovies (see page 6) and stir them into the softened butter until smooth. Taste for salt—you probably don't need any more, but still. Slice the celery into sticks and cut the radishes in halves or quarters, sprinkle them lightly with salt, and serve with the anchovy butter and cool drinks.

Variations: In their seasons, raw snap peas, fennel, cherry tomatoes, cucumbers, peppers, or cauliflower can replace the radishes and celery.

THICK TOAST WITH KALE, CARDOONS, GARLIC, AND ANCHOVIES

This one I learned from Benedetta Vitali's book *Soffritto.* It's a winter recipe and eating it, you start to think that even though ripe tomatoes and sweet peppers are months away, it's going to be okay—with anchovies and olive oil, you'll make it.

I had the chance to cook with Benedetta, the acclaimed Florentine chef, when she visited Chez Panisse some years back. I was explaining to the cooks at our meeting that though the cardoon season had ended, we'd just gotten the first box of tender artichokes, so we would be using those with the kale instead. Benedetta sat up straight and strict, denying absolutely that such a substitution could be made.

"Non è possibile!" she cried. "It must be cardoons!"

"Benedetta, *mi scusi,* but aren't they very similar? They are cousins and they both like anchovies, no?" I tried. She looked unmoved. I tried some more. "These *carciofi* are very good."

"Va bene," she said and shrugged the kind of Italian shrug that means, "You are clearly beyond helping and now I am going to have to watch you fail and will have to rescue you. Oh, how I am tired."

Makes 6 hearty toasts

2 cardoon stalks (or use artichoke hearts prepared as on page 71; Benedetta won't know)

½ lemon (or a splash of any vinegar that isn't balsamic)

Kosher or sea salt

1 bunch lacinato kale, stems stripped away and discarded, leaves washed, drained, and roughly chopped

1 almond-size garlic clove, pounded (see page 6)

2 teaspoons red wine vinegar

3 tablespoons good olive oil, plus more to drizzle

Freshly ground black pepper

6 slices of good, rustic bread, sliced ¾-inch thick (stale bread is fine)

One 2-ounce can anchovy fillets (10 to 12 fillets), drained, fillets cut in half lengthwise

Parmesan, for grating

To prepare the cardoons, have a bowl of water at hand for the stalks to land in once trimmed and squeeze the lemon into it to keep them from turning brown. Cut the ends off one of the stalks, then cut it in half crosswise so that it is more manageable. Using either a paring knife or vegetable peeler, trim off any leaves and spiny edges and peel the outside of the stalks to remove the tough fibers. Rub the fuzz from the insides and submerge the halves in the acidulated water. Repeat with the other stalk.

Bring a medium pot of water to a boil, add salt till you can taste it, and boil the cardoons until very tender. Sometimes they cook quickly, but usually they don't, so after 10 minutes or so, poke a piece with a paring knife. If it's hard, keep cooking. If it feels tender, slice off a little piece and taste it to be sure. Be patient—you want them to be tender. Drain the cardoons and set aside to cool.

Heat the oven to 450°F.

Bring a medium pot of water to a boil (the cardoon water can be bitter, so start fresh). Add salt and then the kale. Boil until tender, about 10 minutes, but taste to be sure. Drain and set aside.

Meanwhile, make a vinaigrette by stirring the pounded garlic with the vinegar and olive oil. Crack in some black pepper.

Place the slices of bread on a tray and toast in the oven until crisp and lightly browned on the outside but still soft in the center, about 5 minutes (a timer helps). Cut the cardoons across into ½-inch-thick slices and, in a mixing bowl, dress them and the kale with the vinaigrette and a pinch of salt. Spread the mixture onto the toasts. Distribute the strips of anchovy among the toasts and return them to the oven for a couple of minutes, just to warm everything up. Place the toasts on a platter, douse with plenty of good olive oil, shave or grate Parmesan on top, and serve warm.

Variation: If you can't find or deal with cardoons or artichokes, replace them with boiled-tender slices of celery, or just use the kale solo.

GREEN BEANS AND POTATOES
WITH ANCHOVIES, TARRAGON, AND DILL

Potatoes might seem kinda beige and dumb with blank looks on their mute, baffled faces, but there's more behind those weird eyes than you might think. Though spuds do fall roughly into two un-tasty-sounding categories, waxy and floury, varietal and seasonal differences are many. Luckily, it matters more for frying, where things can get tricky, and here we are boiling potatoes—more forgiving. If your potatoes are a little floury and breaky, they will mix with the dressing in this warm green bean salad, making it almost creamy. Waxy types will remain more discrete and make for a more delicate dish.

I need to come clean here about my herb use: I did too much dill. I was young and foolish and it's sad, but sometimes it seemed like there was no other option. It wasn't good for me or my career, and I eventually kicked. But as Tom Waits says to Iggy Pop as he lights up in Jim Jarmusch's film *Coffee and Cigarettes,* "The beauty of quitting is that now that I've quit it, I can handle 'em. 'Cause I quit, y'know? [They're] just like jewelry. I don't even inhale. You wanna join me?"

Iggy does.

Makes 6 servings

1 pound yellow-fleshed potatoes (Bintje or German Butterballs are ideal)

Kosher or sea salt

1 almond-size garlic clove

One 2-ounce can anchovy fillets (10 to 12 fillets), drained

1 teaspoon Dijon mustard

1 teaspoon red wine vinegar

Juice of ½ lemon

Freshly ground black pepper

¼ cup good olive oil

¾ pound green beans, stem ends snapped off

4 to 6 dill sprigs, main stems removed

3 tarragon sprigs, leaves picked from stems

If the skins seem thick and tough, peel the potatoes. Otherwise, leave the skin on and cut them into bite-size chunks. Put the potatoes in a pot, cover with cold water, add salt, and bring to a boil. Lower to a simmer, stir once to prevent sticking, and taste the water for salt. Cook until a knife slides in easily—taste a chunk to be sure it's cooked through. Drain. Return the potatoes to the pot they were boiled in and cover with a lid to keep warm.

Meanwhile, put a pot of water on for boiling the green beans and make the dressing: Pound the garlic with a pinch of salt until nearly liquid. Add the anchovies and pound to a paste. Add the mustard, red wine vinegar, lemon juice, and black pepper, then stir in the olive oil.

When the water is boiling, salt it well and add the green beans. Roughly chop the dill and tarragon and stir them into the dressing. The green beans should be done in about 4 minutes, but taste one to be sure and keep going if needed. When tender, drain the green beans and put them in a mixing bowl with the potatoes, the dressing, and a pinch of salt. Grind in some black pepper, toss to mix well, taste, adjust, and serve.

GREEN BEAN AND FRISÉE SALAD WITH ALMOND AND ANCHOVY DRESSING

This salad started with egg and anchovy dressing, a recipe that I'd already published. Delicious, I knew, but, unsure of the protocol on re-publishing my own recipes, I asked my wise editor how to handle it. Readers like it, she said, if you update it, bring in something new. I admit that I rolled my purist eyes, bemoaning a world increasingly devoid of meaningful tradition. Working up a head of steam, I went on to mourn the loss of the patience to stay on one topic for even a minute. "Isn't perfect good enough? Does it have to be perfect *and* new?" I cried, beseeching. It was as I raised my fists heavenward and began to shake them that it occurred to me that my editor, and readers, are quite right. Maybe there is something new and good! Why use eggs in the land of almonds (farmers in California grow a *lot* of almonds)? Almonds do something similar to what eggs do in dressing: give it weight, viscosity, and cling. Sherry vinegar is natural with almonds, so I switched that in for the lemon juice, added a pinch of smoky pimentón de la Vera, and came up with a whole new effect. Thank you, readers!

Makes 6 servings

Kosher or sea salt

½ pound green beans, stem ends snapped off

2 heaping tablespoons toasted almonds (see page 14)

1 almond-size garlic clove

4 to 6 anchovy fillets (half of a 2-ounce can)

Freshly ground black pepper

¼ teaspoon pimentón de la Vera (optional, but smoky-good)

1 scant teaspoon red wine vinegar

1 scant teaspoon sherry vinegar

5 tablespoons good olive oil

1 large head frisée, green leaf-tips trimmed away and core removed so that leaves are loose (romaine, escarole, Belgian endive, or curly endive are also good choices)

Bring a pot of water to a boil and add salt till it tastes right (see page 8). Drop the green beans in the water and cook until tender, about 4 minutes, but taste one to be sure. Drain the green beans and spread on a platter to cool.

Roughly crush the almonds in a mortar and pestle. Set the almonds aside and, using the mortar and pestle, pound the garlic with a pinch of salt until nearly liquid. Add the anchovies and pound to a paste. Add half of the almonds back in and pound to a paste again. Grind in some black pepper and stir in the pimentón de la Vera, if using, and the vinegars. Stir in the olive oil, taste, correct, and set aside.

When you are ready to serve the salad, toss the green beans and frisée in a mixing bowl with most of the dressing, the remaining almonds, and a pinch of salt until well coated. Taste a leaf, correct for salt or a little more of the reserved dressing, and serve.

Variation: Thank goodness my former coworker Samin Nosrat took one for the team and got in her kitchen with a pot of boiling water, a carton of eggs, and a timer and figured out once and for all the how-long-to-boil-an-egg-to-get-it-just-right thing. Samin shows us, in her essential cookbook Salt, Fat, Acid, Heat, *the results of 1 minute in the swim, then 2, 3, and so on. Turns out, for the egg version of this dressing I like a 7-minute egg—set white, thick, almost solid yolk—a perfect vehicle for anchovies to ride. Replace the almonds with a 7-minute egg, the sherry vinegar with lemon juice, add Parmesan, and it's Caesar dressing.*

ANCHOÏADE DE CROZE

I like to think of Austin de Croze, turn-of-the-century culinary chronicler
and compiler of spoof occult calendars, sitting around drinking with fellow
gastronome Curnonsky, both of them high on pastis or laudanum or just
the Provençal light and dreaming up new sauces like this anchoïade. They
are in a garden, taking their leisure on a long afternoon, dressed mostly in
ruffled white. The scent of orange blossoms floats by as wasps buzz the fig
tree and red peppers ripen on the vine. There are drinks of course, and a
tray of walnuts for cracking, and old Curnonsky, back from a holiday in
Spain, produces a tin of anchovies from one pocket and a key to open it
from the other. That's all it takes: Austin, potent, wandering, and wondering
what else might appear from those deep and fecund pockets, is struck with
inspiration.

"Anchovies! Walnuts! Peppers! Figs! Curnonsky, this is crazy, my friend,
but put all of them together in the mortar! Pound in garlic, of course," he says,
shrugging. "We're French, after all! And olive oil, for it is a sauce, and . . .
and the orange flower water, because I am a genius!"

This *is* a genius sauce, a weird and wonderful thing that works though it
shouldn't, but go slow with the orange flower water or it gets a little *parfum-
erie*. Classic to slather onto toasted rustic bread slices, but great wherever else
you think it might go . . . I'm thinking grilled vegetables and meats, lamb
especially.

3 or 4 dried or ripe fresh figs
(Black Mission and Kudota are
wonderful)

Cooking oil, olive or vegetable

Kosher or sea salt

1 red bell pepper

1 teaspoon red wine vinegar or
sherry vinegar

¼ teaspoon fennel seeds, toasted
(see page 14)

1 almond-size garlic clove

One 2-ounce can anchovy fillets
(10 to 12 fillets), drained

¼ cup almonds, peeled (or not)
(see page 15), and lightly toasted
(see page 14)

½ cup good olive oil

2 tablespoons finely chopped
parsley

Drops of orange flower water
(optional)

If you're using dried figs, trim the stem ends and cut them in halves. Pour boiling water over the figs in a small bowl and soak until soft, about 30 minutes. Discard the water and finely chop the figs.

If using fresh figs, heat the oven to 425°F. Trim off the stem ends and cut the figs in half. In a small skillet or baking dish, toss the figs with a coating of cooking oil and a pinch of salt and roast until ready to fall apart, about 20 minutes. When cool enough to handle, chop the figs.

Meanwhile, roast and finely chop the bell pepper (see page 88). Dress with a pinch of salt and the vinegar and set aside.

To make the sauce, I go start to finish with the mortar and pestle. (You can also use a food processor or blender, but grind the fennel seeds and pound the garlic and anchovies before proceeding.) Crush the fennel seeds to powder, then add the garlic and a pinch of salt and pound to a paste. Add the anchovies, pound to a paste again, then add the almonds and keep pounding until a chunky paste forms. Stir in the figs and roasted pepper, the olive oil and parsley. Add 2 drops of orange flower water, if using, stir well, and taste, adjusting for salt, garlic, and the perfume of an orange tree in blossom.

CRISP TOAST-BITE WITH BASIL LEAF, ANCHOVY FILLET, SAMBAL OELEK DAB, AND A PEANUT

This fucked-up Frankensnack happened when I was on vacation. I might have had a sip of this or a tiny toke of that and this creation is maybe evidence of why I shouldn't CUI. Or maybe it's delicious proof that I *should* cook under the influence. The "toast-bite" that I used was a cheesy, bright orange, square little cracker, a well-known product with a Z in its name. I had a "toast-bite" habit as a kid and am completely over it, just about. I don't bring regimens along on vacation though, and so discovered that it is possible for me to eat just one, or so, "toast-bites," provided they are embellished with very adult ingredients like basil, hot chilies, and anchovies. And a peanut.

Serves and keeps on serving

Assemble the titular ingredients into little canapés. Eat them, probably with cold beer. Try not to eat more. Fail.

ROASTED SWEET PEPPER
AND EGG SALAD WITH ANCHOVIES,
OLIVES, AND CAPERS

My friend Ignacio Mattos cooked with me at Chez
Panisse for a spell before rolling over to the other coast
and making it big in New York. Ignacio has developed a
brilliance for creating dishes that simultaneously comfort and
surprise, plates that visually pop and are flat-out delicious. Every time I eat
at Estela, I can't wait to hurry back to Berkeley and start unashamedly chan-
neling him, spinning up bright green sauces and turning salads on their
heads.

I was stumbling around the making of this roasted sweet pepper salad
with a friend keeping me company in the kitchen when he asked me what was
wrong.

"I'm trying to do it like Ignacio, but I keep forgetting and doing it right side
up," I said, picking olives from atop the peppers, where I'd just sprinkled them
fancifully, and tucking them under with everything else. "It's harder than you
think."

"Is it a South American thing?" he asked.

"It might be a New York thing," I said.

"Do those work in Berkeley?" he asked.

"I miss New York," I sighed, heading to the table. "Let's eat."

3 large red, orange, or yellow bell peppers

Good olive oil

1 teaspoon red wine vinegar

Kosher or sea salt

6 eggs

1 almond-size garlic clove, pounded (see page 6)

One 2-ounce can anchovy fillets (10 to 12 fillets), drained and chopped

2 tablespoons capers, well soaked if salt-packed, rinsed if brined, chopped

2 tablespoons chopped parsley

½ teaspoon chopped oregano or marjoram leaves

Freshly ground black pepper

¼ cup black olives, Niçoise or another type that isn't Kalamata, pitted and torn in half

Roast the peppers: Set them, just as they are, atop a gas burner turned up high. As each side chars, use tongs to turn to the next side, top and bottom, until the skin is blackened all over. (Alternatively, rub the peppers with cooking oil and roast them on a baking sheet in a 450°F oven or under a broiler until charred and collapsing.) Put the peppers in a bag or covered container and set aside to steam for 20 minutes. Keeping the peppers as whole as possible, peel the charred skin off them with your fingers, pull off the stem ends, and remove the seeds and membranes. Give the peppers a quick rinse, pat them dry, and dress with 2 tablespoons olive oil, the vinegar, and ½ teaspoon salt. Set aside.

Meanwhile, bring a small saucepan of water to a boil, add the eggs, and cook for 9 minutes for a set but not overcooked, chop-pable yolk. Cool, peel, and coarsely chop the eggs, or push them through a spider. In a medium bowl, combine the eggs, garlic, anchovies, capers, parsley, oregano, 3 tablespoons olive oil, and salt and pepper to taste.

Spoon the egg salad onto plates or a platter and smooth into low mounds. Make like the Easter Bunny and hide the eggs, covering them neatly with the roasted peppers. Ignacio would tuck the olives under there, too, but I always forget and polka dot them on top. Stripe the salad with olive oil.

PENNE ALLA TUNA-NESCA

Pasta alla puttanesca is a classic that shouldn't be messed with. And yet . . . what if it's summer and you want to make it a little chunkier, with less pasta, more stuff, and fresh ripe tomatoes instead of the typical canned? And then there's fresh albacore tuna, cooked slowly with fennel in olive oil, that fits in so Nice with the capers, olives, and anchovies. Add plenty of herbs, and oil from the tuna, and on a hot night you'll eat it, warm and spicy, with cool red wine.

This recipe has some steps and takes some time, but doesn't use the oven so it won't be too hot in the kitchen. The tuna in oil can be cooked ahead—handily, it lasts for days in the fridge, getting, some say, better—and the tomato concassé (peeled, seeded, and chopped fresh tomatoes) can be made earlier in the day. Even making the sauce entirely and popping it in the fridge to heat up later while you boil the pasta would be okay.

Makes 4 or 5 servings

¾ pound fresh albacore tuna, cut in inch-thick chunks

Kosher or sea salt

½ teaspoon fennel seeds, toasted (see page 14) and ground nearly to powder

½ teaspoon coriander seeds, toasted (see page 14) and ground nearly to powder

Freshly ground black pepper

Olive oil (doesn't need to be best, salad grade—using part vegetable oil is fine, too)

¾ pound ripe tomatoes

1 small red onion, thinly sliced

One 2-ounce can anchovy fillets (10 to 12 fillets), drained

2 garlic cloves, finely chopped

Crushed red pepper flakes

2 tablespoons capers, well soaked if salt-packed, rinsed if brined, chopped

½ cup little black olives, Niçoise or another type that isn't Kalamata, pitted and roughly chopped

1 pound penne

2 tablespoons chopped parsley

1 teaspoon finely chopped oregano or marjoram leaves (or dried oregano to taste)

Sprinkle the tuna all over with a generous ½ teaspoon salt, the fennel, coriander, and black pepper. Pat everything onto the fish and set aside at room temperature for 15 to 30 minutes.

Over low heat, warm a skillet that will fit the tuna as snugly as possible and swirl in oil to coat the bottom. Fit the tuna pieces into the skillet and add enough oil to come nearly halfway up their sides. Cook slowly, nudging the pieces once to avoid sticking. As it cooks, the tuna will turn pale and opaque. Lower the heat if things get rowdy at all, and turn the pieces over after 3 to 4 minutes to cook the other side The tuna is done when the middle is just set and not yet entirely opaque. Break a piece open to check, and remember that it will keep cooking a little off the heat. Cool the tuna and oil separately, then reunite them until you're ready to carry on. Refrigerate if it's going to be a while, of course.

Put a big pot of cold water on to boil for the pasta. Add salt till it tastes right (page 8). This water can be used for making the tomato concasee and then for boiling the pasta.

To make tomato concassé, prepare a bowl of ice water, and then slip the tomatoes into the pot of boiling water. Fish them out when the skins feel loose to the pinch, around 30 seconds, and drop them into the ice water to cool. With a paring knife, cut out the green stem end and pull off the skin. If it's very stuck, drop the offender back in the pot for a few seconds more. Cut the tomatoes in half at their equators and gently squeeze, cut side facing down, to get the seeds out. Cut the halves into chunky dice, sprinkle with a little salt, and set aside.

Heat a large skillet on high and add 3 tablespoons of the oil you cooked the tuna in, then the onion and a light sprinkle of salt (the capers, anchovies, and olives will add saltiness later). Stir the onion until it gets going, then turn to medium and cook, stirring occasionally, until soft and well browned, 15 to 20 minutes. Add the anchovies and cook a minute or two, so that they melt into the onion, then add the garlic and red pepper flakes, stirring and smelling the good, not burning, garlic. Add the tomatoes, capers, and olives. Raise the heat to bring the sauce to a simmer and cook until the tomatoes have just lost their rawness, about 4 minutes. Crumble in the tuna, stir, taste the sauce, and adjust as needed.

Meanwhile, boil the penne to al dente and drain, reserving a cupful of cooking water in case the sauce needs thinning. Mix the pasta, parsley, and oregano or marjoram into the sauce and stir/toss to coat well. Taste, adjust with the reserved water if needed for more flow, and serve. No cheese.

Variation: Use a 5-ounce can of tuna, drained, instead of the home-cooked albacore.

PAN BAGNAT

If, like me, you used to *like* it when your pb&j got smashed in your lunch box, actually preferred the jelly-marinated and peanut butter–infused slices that resulted from a couple of hours wedged under a math book, then you'll probably love pan bagnat. Somewhere between muffaletta and panzanella, pan bagnat is a summer sandwich you build, then crush, like a sandcastle.

Makes 4 to 6 servings

1 almond-size garlic clove

Kosher or sea salt

One 2-ounce can anchovy fillets (10 to 12 fillets), drained

1 teaspoon red wine vinegar

Freshly ground black pepper

¼ cup good olive oil

A rustic loaf of bread

3 or 4 hard-boiled eggs, sliced

1 large red, orange, or yellow bell pepper, seeded and thinly sliced

1 large ripe tomato, thinly sliced

1 cucumber, thinly sliced

1 small red onion, thinly sliced

1 cup black olives, preferably Niçoise, pitted and roughly chopped

1 cup basil leaves

2 handfuls arugula leaves (optional)

One 5-ounce can tuna, drained, or albacore cooked in olive oil (see page 90; optional)

To make the dressing, pound the garlic and a pinch of salt with a mortar and pestle until nearly liquid. Add the anchovies and pound to a paste. Add the vinegar and grind in some black pepper, then stir in the olive oil. Set the dressing aside.

Split the loaf lengthwise. If it is a dense-crumbed loaf, you may want to tear out some of the insides. Give the dressing a good stir and spread about half of it on the cut sides of the loaf halves. Layer on the hard-boiled egg slices, pepper, tomato, cucumber, red onion, olives, basil, and arugula leaves, if using, onto one half of the loaf. Add the tuna, if using, drizzle evenly with the remaining dressing, and top with the other half of the loaf. Wrap the sandwich tightly in plastic wrap, waxed paper, or foil and press under a math book, or other weight, for at least 30 minutes and up to 4 hours. If the juices leak out onto your homework, well, that's your excuse for why you didn't turn it in.

Variation: When I don't feel like eating tuna, but want a similar substantive ingredient, I add pan-roasted slices of eggplant (page 29) instead.

TONNATO SAUCE

Tonnato sauce always makes me think of the great Rossellini movie *Stromboli*. Not the part where Ingrid Bergman is overcome by sulfurous volcanic fumes, but rather the incredible and harrowing tuna-fishing sequence. The tuna they catch are enormous and dangerous, and probably the hardy fishermen aren't thinking about mayonnaise-y sauce, but I swear I saw a caper bush on a rocky slope as Ingrid cries, *"Dio, Dio mio!"* and I started craving tonnato through my tears.

Somewhere between tartar sauce and a sun-soaked Mediterranean island, tonnato is traditionally meant for smearing on slices of roasted veal, but I like it smeared everywhere else.

Makes 2 cups

1 almond-size garlic clove, pounded (see page 6)

One 2-ounce can anchovy fillets (10 to 12 fillets), drained

1 egg yolk

½ teaspoon Dijon mustard

Juice of half a lemon

1 cup mild olive oil (or a mixture of equal parts olive oil and neutral vegetable oil . . . grapeseed, canola, or similar)

2 tablespoons capers, well soaked if salt-packed, rinsed if brined, chopped

2 tablespoons chopped parsley

½ teaspoon chopped marjoram leaves

Freshly ground black pepper

Cayenne or Marash-type pepper to taste

One 5-ounce can oil-packed tuna, drained, or albacore cooked in olive oil, crumbled (see page 90)

With either a mortar and pestle or a cutting board and chef's knife, mash the garlic and anchovy fillets into a paste. Put the paste in a small mixing bowl and add the egg yolk, mustard, and lemon juice. Stir with a whisk and begin adding the olive oil, drop by drop at first, then in a slow stream as the mixture thickens and forms an emulsion. When it gets very thick and shiny, thin it with a splash of water and continue whisking in the remaining olive oil. Stir in the capers, parsley, marjoram, a few grinds of black pepper, Cayenne pepper, and tuna. The texture should be more creamy than bouncy, so thin with a splash more water if needed. The tuna chunks will break up the more you stir—you can decide how chunky or smooth you want the sauce to be. Taste for salt and lemon, adjust, and serve with:

* *Sliced ripe tomatoes and/or cucumbers (summer)*
* *Grilled or roasted yellow, orange, or red bell peppers (summer)*
* *Boiled green beans (summer), cauliflower (fall/winter), or artichokes (spring)*
* *Hard-cooked eggs*
* *Boiled, peeled, and chilled wild-caught shrimp*
* *Poached or grilled chicken*
* *Cold slices of pork loin, pork shoulder roast, or roast beef*

BAGNA CAUDA SALAD
WITH OPTIONAL TRUFFLE UPGRADE

Typically at my dinner parties, everyone eats standing around for at least part of the time. People get hungry, smelling enticing smells while they drink and talk in the kitchen, and start tearing into loaves of bread, dipping and smearing, and looking for where to put olive pits and radish tops. Kids' mouths go green as a gang of them get to work with the chips on a bowl of guacamole. If I've made bagna cauda, it goes fast too. Bagna cauda—hot fragrant anchovy sauce to dip raw turnips into—might sound, to some, more like the end of the party than the beginning, but my experience tells a different story. Everyone, even the kids, loves bagna cauda.

Sometimes, however, the company isn't right for dips and we need to eat it, whatever it is, another way. Times like when the guests are awkward with each other, meeting for the first time. Or it might be that it's too cold in the backyard and we want to come in and sit, and the table is too big for everyone to reach. Or maybe I'm just feeling fancy. So I put this dip on plates, and everybody gets one! It's more polite, sure, but no less fun, and as a bonus it helps to avoid squabbles and stains.

Makes 6 servings

2 almond-size garlic cloves

Kosher or sea salt

One 2-ounce can anchovy fillets
(10 to 12 fillets), drained

1 tablespoon unsalted butter

Good olive oil

1 black truffle (optional)

1½ pounds tender vegetables, such as white turnips, fennel, carrots, rutabaga, kohlrabi, radishes, artichokes, Jerusalem artichokes, celery

1 teaspoon white wine vinegar

1 tablespoon finely chopped parsley (if not using truffle)

Using a mortar and pestle, pound the garlic with a pinch of salt until nearly liquid, then add the anchovies and pound to a paste. In a small skillet or saucepan, over low heat, melt the butter with 2 tablespoons olive oil. Add the garlic and anchovy mixture and cook, keeping the heat very low and stirring and mashing the anchovies occasionally, until it all melts together and smells really good, about 10 minutes. Add the black truffle, if using, and keep warm while you assemble the salad.

Using a very sharp knife or mandoline, carefully slice the vegetables as thinly as you can. For some things, like carrots, a vegetable peeler is good for making thin strips. Round shapes should be cut in half and set on the flat side for further slicing. Put the sliced vegetables in a large bowl and dress with salt, the vinegar, and 2 tablespoons olive oil. Toss in the parsley if you're not using truffle. Taste, adjust, and spread onto salad plates or a platter, not piled up, so that the bagna cauda can get everywhere. Spoon the warm bagna cauda over the salad and serve.

SPAGHETTI ALLA BOTTARGA

When I eat bottarga, I prefer bottarga di muggine. There's no way to say that without sounding snotty, so, sorry. Bottarga is salted and pressed fish roe, from either tuna or, the kind I like, gray mullet. Mullet bottarga has a flavor like anchovies, but subtler, less salty, and a little sweeter. Unlike anchovies, the price of bottarga ranges from expensive to really expensive.

I was in a restaurant in Torino the first time I had spaghetti alla bottarga. The day before, I'd never heard of it, but after sampling half a dozen kinds at a food show, I was an instantly opinionated enthusiast who preferred the mullet. A group of us were eating together and as we waited for our primos, a famous chef at our table sent back the bread, sweetly yet aggressively asking that it be grilled for us. She wanted to douse toasts with the tin of newly pressed olive oil she had in her purse: a gift from a fan, a happy hazard of her position. I was embarrassed to have to translate her request—refusal, I knew, was not something she could imagine—but quite eager for it to be granted: she *could* imagine sending *me* into the kitchen to do the grilling, if that's what it took. They didn't want to do it, possibly because they didn't actually have a grill, but somehow finally did.

Any awkwardness was soon soothed with great green glugs of the best olive oil I have ever had, and by the spaghetti that followed, fragrant of the sea and tasting of a sweetness that only the combination of salt and time can bring.

Kosher or sea salt

1 pound spaghetti

1 almond-size garlic clove

1 ounce grated bottarga di muggine, plus more for the table (see note)

¼ cup olive oil

Bring a large pot of water to a boil. Add salt till it tastes right (see page 8), and then the spaghetti, stirring occasionally. Meanwhile, pound the garlic with a pinch of salt and stir it, the grated bottarga, and the olive oil in a bowl big enough to hold the spaghetti. Start tasting pieces of spaghetti at 9 minutes and when it is done the way you like it, drain it, saving a cupful of water. Stir the spaghetti with the garlic-bottarga-olive oil mixture and a splash of the pasta water. Taste and correct for salt and add a bit more water if it needs some flow. Serve right away. No cheese for this one, but consider passing more grated bottarga at the table, because sometimes a lot is just enough.

Note: Bottarga is available at specialty stores and, as if I need to tell you, online.

FRIED ANCHOVY
AND SAGE STANDWICHETTES

So-called because they taste better eaten standing up in the kitchen, these crunch-puffy little bites pack enough serious flavor to strut alongside strong cocktails, but have a charming elegance that capers equally well with cold white wine, beer, or dry sherry.

Makes 12 and can be easily doubled

¼ cup dry white wine, plus more as needed

¼ cup all-purpose flour

6 anchovy fillets (half a 2-ounce can)

12 thumbnail-size cubes of bread cut from a rustic loaf (day-old works great)

12 sage leaves

12 wooden toothpicks

Frying oil (canola, grapeseed, rice bran, and so on)

Favorite cold wine, beer, sherry, or cocktail (semi-optional)

Make the batter: In a medium mixing bowl, whisk the wine into the flour until smooth. It should be slightly thicker than un-whipped cream. Thin with wine or water as needed. Set aside.

Cut the anchovy fillets in half lengthwise. Wrap a cube of bread with one of the fillet halves, then wrap it with a sage leaf and secure the standwichette with a toothpick. Wrap the rest of the bread cubes the same way.

Heat at least an inch of oil in a small skillet or saucepan over medium heat until it shimmers but doesn't smoke and a small drop of batter sizzles with vigor but not frenzied vigor (about 350°F if you're using a thermometer). Check the batter consistency and adjust if it has thickened up.

Put half the standwichettes into the batter and turn them to coat completely. Lift them by their toothpicks, let drip for a few seconds, then place into the hot oil. Fry until golden brown, grabbing their toothpicks with tongs to turn them in the oil if necessary to get all sides. Drain on paper towels and pass them around the kitchen while you have a drink and fry the next batch.

GRILLED ANCHOÏADE-SOAKED BREAD WITH EGGS AND HERBS

My sons ate a hell of a lot of bagels growing up: smeared with cream cheese or peanut butter, griddled with a fried egg, or as the bread for their lunchbox sandwiches. For a long time, I ate them too, and for a long time, that was okay. Until it wasn't: I started to notice a connection between bagel eating and the doughy dad-belly that bumped the counter in front of me as I spread on the schmear. Something had to change. So I did some carbo-triage, sorting into three categories: never eat, almost never eat, and never stop eating. Good, rustic bread grilled after a soaking of oily garlic and anchovy paste is too good to ever give up.

Makes generous appetizers for 6

4 eggs

2 savory sprigs or 4 thyme sprigs, leaves picked from stems

1 almond-size garlic clove

Kosher or sea salt

One 2-ounce can anchovy fillets (10 to 12 fillets), drained

¼ cup good olive oil, plus a little to drizzle

1 rustic baguette

Freshly ground black pepper

2 big handfuls of a mixture of arugula and parsley, basil, or mint leaves, whole if small, otherwise roughly chopped

Half a lemon

Bring a saucepan of water to a boil. Gently add the eggs and lower the heat so it keeps boiling, but not ferociously. Cook for 8 minutes—this will give you fully set whites with a solid yet still soft-ish yolk. Drain the eggs and cool them in cold water.

Meanwhile, make the anchoïade: Finely chop or pound the savory or thyme with a mortar and pestle until well mashed. Add the garlic with a pinch of salt and pound until nearly liquid, then add the anchovies and pound to a paste. Peel one of the hard-boiled eggs and push it through a sieve or spider and into the anchoïade. Stir in the olive oil. Split the loaf of bread lengthwise and smear the anchoïade evenly on the cut sides and let it soak in while you get a hot grill ready (or heat the oven to 450°F).

Peel, slice, and season the remaining eggs with salt and black pepper.

Grill the bread, cut side down, until browned and crispy (or bake on a baking sheet, cut side up, until the same, 8 to 10 minutes). Grill the crust side to crisp

it up as well, then cut the bread into segments and divide the sliced eggs among them. Dress the arugula and herbs with a drizzle of olive oil, a squeeze of lemon, salt, and black pepper and scatter over the toasts.

CAESAR'S GOUGÈRES

A poet I know asked me to teach him a good solid egg dish, one that he could make in the morning for a date who had stayed the night. I blushed into my keyboard and emailed back that I had just the thing, a leftover pasta and greens frittata that involves a deliciously exciting moment when things can get messy. It's squiggly, satisfying, and once you get the flip-over under control, sexy.

It turned out that Tommy Pico was looking for more than just a dish to set the hook in last night's hook-up. He was getting into the kitchen to, as he put it, "create a new world of metaphors and language for myself." He could have chosen any number of jargon-loaded crafts—trimming topiary, upholstering, keeping bees—that would expand his word world, but he chose cooking for the real-life perks of money saving and better eating. He then admitted that this would be his first experience with cooking eggs, literally any style! I got to guide him through cracking his first egg ever! I was nervous, like when baby takes his first steps, but he did not stumble. I think that if I'd known of his, um, ineggsperience, I would probably have started with a fry, scramble, boil, poach primer. He'll probably get around to the basics himself, now that the gateway to egg world has been opened wide.

Next time Tommy and I cook together, I think I'll suggest Caesar's Gougères, a sort of cheese puff/Caesar dressing mash up. There's plenty of egg in them and they're so hot, decadent, and irresistible that I'll bet he sees them as more night-of than morning-after.

½ cup whole milk

8 tablespoons (1 stick) unsalted butter

½ teaspoon kosher or sea salt

1 cup all-purpose flour

4 eggs

1¼ cups grated Parmesan

2 almond-size garlic cloves, pounded (see page 6)

One 2-ounce can anchovy fillets (10 to 12 fillets), drained

Freshly ground black pepper

Worcestershire sauce (optional)

1 lemon

Heat the oven to 400°F. Line a baking sheet with parchment paper and find your pastry bag. If you don't have those, it's fine: just skip the parchment, and for dolloping out the gougères, use a plastic bag with the corner cut off, or just use a couple of spoons.

Make the pâte à choux: In a small saucepan, bring the milk and ½ cup water to a boil with the butter and salt. Add the flour all at once, turn off the heat, and stir with a wooden spoon until completely incorporated. Return to very low heat and stir for a few minutes until the dough forms a ball and a film begins to form, and lightly brown, in the saucepan. Remove from the heat, let cool for a couple minutes, then stir in the eggs, one at a time, until completely incorporated. The dough will fall to pieces when you add egg—keep calm and keep stirring; it will pull itself together.

Add the Parmesan, garlic, anchovies, plenty of black pepper, Worcestershire sauce to taste, if using, and the zest and juice from about one quarter of the lemon. Taste the dough and adjust for salt, lemon, cheese, and so on. It will be very sticky.

Scoop the dough into a pastry bag with a plain tip, or no tip, and pipe out balls of dough about the size of a large cherry onto the baking sheet, leaving about an inch between them. Put the gougères in the oven—for proper puff, it is important to not open the oven during the initial 20 minutes of baking. Now you can check them—if they need a bit more browning, bake for another 5 minutes. Serve hot or warm. Gougères reheat well and can be refrigerated (for a few days) or even frozen (for up to a month) for reheating later.

OKONOMIYAKI

Okonomiyaki is a Japanese savory pancake that is a where-have-you-been-hiding, check-every-box, oh-Mommy-the-umami delight that you don't have to be stoned to love. I probably have zero business devising a recipe for it, Mediterranean foodophile that I am, but after my first okonomiyaki the cravings started and my tab at the Japanese place was getting out of hand. I was pretty much forced/delighted to start cooking it and came up with this. I'm sure there are some authentic touches yet to be learned, but hey, the name means grilled "whatever you like" so you can't go too wrong.

That said, some of the more exotic ingredients you really should try to find, and first among them is katsuobushi: dried, smoked, and shaved bonito. Not only does katsuobushi add savor to the batter, but the shavings that you strew over the finished pancake flutter in the heat like church ladies in August. Kewpie mayonnaise and okonomiyaki sauce are often crisscrossed over the pancake, but they form too sweet a partnership for me. I usually skip the Kewpie or use regular mayo, and instead of okonomiyaki sauce mix up some combination of oyster sauce, soy sauce, ketchup, Worcestershire, and chili sauce, depending on what's rattling around on the fridge door shelves. The mountain yam, yamaimo, turns positively goopers when you grate it. It's exciting and adds something texturally, but you could omit it if impossible to find. Finely grated, almost ripe plantain can be substituted successfully.

Makes one ¾-inch, skillet-size pancake that serves 1 stoned, otherwise 4

3 tablespoons cooking oil, olive or vegetable

3 ounces bacon (3 or 4 slices)

4 ounces yamaimo (about a 4 × 2-inch length); or plantain (see headnote)

3 scallions, all the white and most of the green parts, thinly sliced

¾ ounce katsuobushi

¾ pound green cabbage (about a quarter of a standard-size cabbage), cored and thinly sliced

¼ cup chopped kimchi (optional)

1 tablespoon minced or grated ginger

1 loose cup basil leaves or cilantro stems and leaves, roughly chopped

2 eggs

½ teaspoon kosher or sea salt

Freshly ground black pepper

¾ cup all-purpose flour (or rice flour)

Mayonnaise in a squirt bottle, Kewpie or other type (optional)

3 tablespoons okonomiyaki sauce or blend of bottled sauces (see headnote; optional)

2 or 3 sheets nori seaweed, cut in half and thinly sliced

Warm a large skillet over medium-low heat. Add 1 tablespoon of the oil and the bacon, and cook over gentle heat until it's the way you like it: soft, crispy, or in between. Pour the bacon and its fat into a mixing bowl and grate in the ya-maimo. Add three-quarters of the scallions, three-quarters of the katsuobushi, the cabbage, kimchi (if using), ginger, basil or cilantro, eggs, salt, grinding of black pepper, and ¾ cup water and mix well. Sprinkle and stir in the flour until fully incorporated. The batter should look quite chunky and thick, but if it seems too thick and pasty, stir in a splash more water. The batter can be used right away or stored covered in the refrigerator for up to 2 days.

Heat the skillet you cooked the bacon in to medium. Add the remaining 2 tablespoons oil, swirl to coat the skillet, and then add the batter. Spread it smooth with a spatula or the back of a spoon and cook until it begins to brown around the edges and the middle is bubbling and setting up a little, 5 to 6 minutes. Run a knife around the perimeter of the pancake and shake the pan to be sure that it is releasing. If it seems stuck, carefully slip a spatula under to loosen all around. Slide the pancake onto a plate, invert the skillet over it and, using hot pads or kitchen towels to protect your hands, flip it so that the pancake falls back into the skillet. Return to the heat and cook until completely set, another 5 minutes or so. (Alternatively, heat the oven to 400°F and finish cooking the un-flipped pancake in there, but only if your skillet can go in the oven, of course.) Turn the pancake out onto a platter or serve it straight from the skillet, striped with mayonnaise and okonomiyaki sauce, if using, and sprinkled with the nori, the reserved scallions, and the remaining katsuobushi. Wave back.

TAPENADE

If you lined up all the hors d'oeuvres that I've served to guests at home and at restaurants over the years, they would easily reach from here to the bar and back. I've seen all sorts of foolishness—people trying to be polite and eat radishes with a knife and fork, people mistaking raw shell beans for something they can pop in their mouths, people mistaking the dish of spit olive pits for I don't even know what and popping *those* in their mouths. Maybe they just get nervous because they know I'm watching. Savory tapenade on bite-size toasts eliminates any confusion.

Anchovies, some pounded and some chopped, give tapenade an almost creamy texture and enough substance to make it great, spread on warm toasts, and super great if you spread the toasts first with a little fresh goat cheese or ricotta.

Makes 1 cup

1 almond-size garlic clove

One 2-ounce can anchovy fillets (10 to 12 fillets), drained

1 cup pitted and chopped Niçoise or Picholine olives, or a combination of the two

2 tablespoons capers, well soaked if salt-packed, rinsed if brined, chopped

1 tablespoon chopped parsley

1/4 teaspoon finely chopped thyme, sage, marjoram, or oregano leaves

Finely chopped or grated zest of 1/4 lemon

1/4 cup olive oil

Using a mortar and pestle, or with a cutting board and chef's knife, mash the garlic and half the anchovy fillets into a paste. Chop the remaining anchovies. In a small bowl or in the mortar, mix the paste with the chopped anchovies and the olives, capers, parsley, other herbs you are using, lemon zest, and olive oil. Stir well, taste, and adjust as desired (more zest, garlic, oil, and so on).

BIGOLI IN SALSA

I love hearing about the parties that happen in Venice during the famous arts Biennale, getting a vicarious thrill from tales of rooftop affairs at the Peggy Guggenheim with lots of Bellinis, coke, and sex. When Kathleen and I visited Venice with our three young sons, it wasn't quite like that—our thrills were far more pedestrian. One-year-old Liam had just found his footing as a newly upright human, only to lose one shoe right when he finally needed it. Luckily, there's the Rialto Bridge, where hapless parents have been buying replacement shoes for their toddlers from stalls above the canal for seven hundred years. No longer an onerous errand, our shoe shopping was now a picturesque adventure, but Liam held another view. Eager clerks held open the mouths of attractively priced shoes, but he refused to insert his tender foot into any of them, looking horrified into their depths as if there might be sharp teeth hiding beneath their leather tongues. When his shrieks began drawing a crowd, we gave up. But not for long: He would not tolerate being carried or carriaged, not when walking had just become an option. The sight of him hobbling half-shod along the cobblestones—shoe, sock, shoe, wet sock, shoe, squish—propelled us into Upim, an upscale (to us) clothing store that fit into our budget only with the lubrication of desperation. Liam loved Upim, surprisingly willing to slide his damp toes into every shoe offered and settling with stubborn finality on a beautiful blue pair with little number fours on the side and a price tag that made us rethink the gilded gondola ride we'd been contemplating.

Happily, we found a cheap and charming, if brocade-less, version—a traghetto—that would row us across the Grand Canal to the Dorsoduro. We stowed the stroller and though there were benches for sitting, stood, like the seasoned commuters who were our fellow passengers, for the short trip to the other side. Except that they were all facing the traghetto's stern. Jaded, I thought, seen it all, crossed so many canals that they've lost interest. I would never become so hardened to the beauty of this floating city, I thought, growing outraged by their indifference. As we pulled away from shore, the oarsmen turned the traghetto around, as the commuters clearly knew that they would, before starting across. We were the ones facing the wrong way, *ovviamente.* Our foolishness must have distracted one of the oarsmen who, as he maneuvered to avoid colliding with an ornately tasseled real gondola, dropped his oar overboard. He was horribly embarrassed, *mortificato,* and I would have felt sorry for him had he not, lunging for his drifting oar, stumbled on the stroller and into Milo, nearly knocking him into the murky, churning canal.

"*O Dio!*" he said.

"*Sì,*" I agreed, and, stepping gratefully ashore at last, added, "*Grazie Dio.*"

We'd planned to wander the *cicchetti* bars for dinner, snacking and drinking our way among the bridges and canals, but now that seemed too ambitious, so we found a nearby trattoria with pizzas for the boys and, *grazie Dio,* pungent plates of *bigoli* in salsa for Kathleen and me.

Makes 4 servings

¼ cup olive oil	Kosher or sea salt
1 medium yellow onion, thinly sliced	One 2-ounce can anchovy fillets (10 to 12 fillets), drained

1 pound whole wheat bigoli or spaghetti (see note)

½ teaspoon chopped marjoram leaves

2 tablespoons capers, well soaked if salt-packed, rinsed if brined, chopped

Juice from half a lemon

1 tablespoon chopped parsley

Heat a large skillet to high and add the olive oil and right away the onion. Sprinkle lightly with salt—the anchovies will add salinity—and stir. Turn the heat to medium-low once things get going and stir in the anchovies. Cook, stirring occasionally and splashing in water as needed to prevent excessive browning, until the onion is very soft and the anchovies have melted into it, about 20 minutes.

Meanwhile, bring a large pot water to a boil and add salt till it tastes right (page 8). Add the pasta, stirring well immediately and then occasionally as it cooks.

Add the marjoram, capers, and lemon juice to the skillet when the pasta is nearly done (taste a piece to know when). Drain the pasta, reserving ½ cup or so of the water, and add the pasta to the skillet. Toss in the parsley and stir to coat well, adding cooking water as needed to achieve some flow. Eat hot.

Note: Bigoli *is a handmade whole wheat pasta that is hand-cranked through a very cool bronze extruder tube; if you have one, go for it! If not, whole grain spaghetti, wheat or other, works well here.*

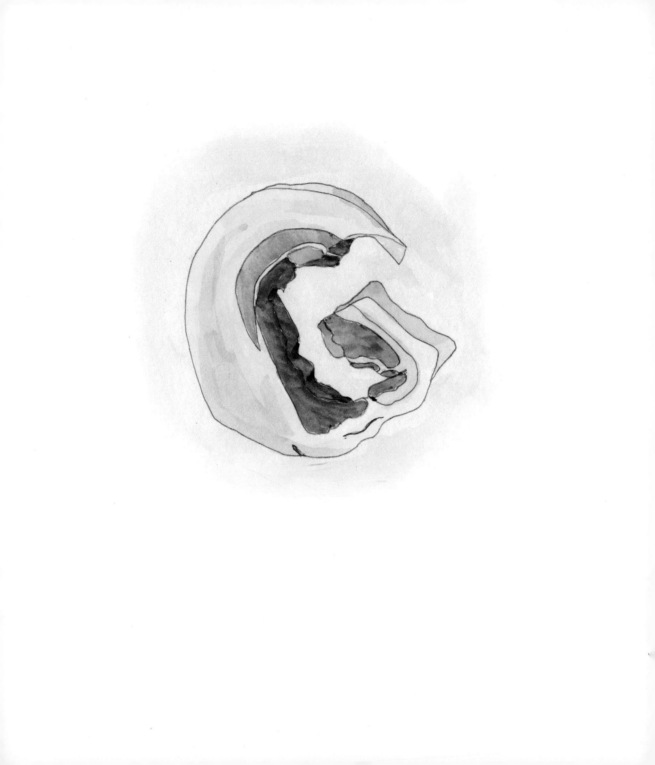

pancetta

In Italy, if a ham is cooked, they say so: prosciutto cotto. If it's a ham that's salt-cured and dried, it's just prosciutto, the default, eaten uncooked. Same with pancetta: It is eaten thinly sliced, not cooked, as an antipasto, and it is lovely that way, but I don't feel tradition bound—here you'll find recipes for cooked pancetta and for variations using other cured porky bits, from old friend bacon to new acquaintance lardo.

Pancetta is made from pork belly, and pork belly is just that: the belly of a pig. Not organ meat, but belly meat, the part of a pig that corresponds to the part of you that you may be rubbing hungrily or resting this book on right now. Transformed with salt, sugar, spices, and curing salt, pancetta is just like bacon, except it isn't smoked. (Curing salt is sodium nitrate and sodium nitrite mixed with salt, and a little pink color so that you don't mistake it for regular salt. The 'trates and 'trites get used up in the curing of the meat, becoming benign nitric oxide.)

Beyond the basic salt-sugar cure, there are many herb and spice flavoring choices for the pancetta-maker. Pancetta can be rolled and cured in a casing for a softer, fattier effect, or it can be left in flat slabs, yielding a drier, nuttier slice.

Thickness of slice is an important aspect of pancetta, and while any pancetta is better than no pancetta, there are definite advantages to being able to choose your slice.

* *For eating as is, uncooked, very thin slices are what you want.*
* *For cooking up crisp and crumble-able, use a slightly thicker slice, thinner than standard sliced bacon.*
* *For sautéing—for greens or beans or pasta, for example—standard bacon thickness, or a little thicker, works best. I generally don't discard the fat rendered from pancetta in the skillet; it's delicious and I'm thrifty: I paid just as much for the fat as the lean, so why not use it?*

PANCETTA

My friend Mike Marshall is mad on the mandolin, from bluegrass to Bach, and you'd think that'd be enough, but on the side, he cooks like crazy too! It's nothing for him to roll out a batch of pillowy gnocchi while roasting a leg of lamb on the Weber and pausing to trill out some riffs, play a perfect crystalline cantata, or start a quick "Pig in a Pen" sing-along. He always has a tin of his homemade Italian cookies or boozy keeping cake on hand, and for years he made his own basement wine: a muscular, palate-challenging red with aromas of every funky-old thing. It's almost a relief that not *every* skill is at Mike's command, but without a doubt the dude likes a project.

Most likely you'll be buying already-made pancetta, but to fully grasp its beautiful simplicity and appreciate the genius of this glorious combination of pork belly, salt, sugar, and spices, I do recommend making a slab in your home kitchen at least once. Mike would. Curing pork belly for pancetta is simple and satisfying. True, pink salt must be found (at your butcher or online) and you'll need to rig up a way to hang the pancetta in your fridge (string and paper clips are what I use), but other than that it really just takes time. It looks pretty bad-ass hanging in the fridge, and since you might as well make plenty while you're at it, this recipe yields enough to impressively gift—you can say "I cured it myself," like you recovered just in time to make a stunning carbonara!

The amounts given here are for curing 3 pounds of belly, but you could cure any amount (though maybe not too small a piece—at least 1½ pounds) using this ratio: the salt amount is 3 percent of the belly by weight, sugar is .33 percent. For pink curing salt, I use cure #2 and halve the amount recommended on the package—it keeps the nice pink color, but leaves the pancetta tasting fresh and not over-cured.

Makes plenty for your recipes, plus some to share

2 tablespoons plus 2 teaspoons kosher or sea salt

1 teaspoon sugar

¼ teaspoon pink curing salt

3 pounds skin-on pork belly, split into 2 squares

Spices and herbs

1 tablespoon fennel seeds, toasted (see page 14) and ground

2 teaspoons coriander seeds, toasted (see page 14) and ground

Freshly ground black pepper

4 juniper berries, ground

4 bay leaves, ground

½ teaspoon crushed red pepper flakes

1 tablespoon finely chopped rosemary leaves

In a small bowl, mix together the salt, sugar, and pink curing salt and coat the belly with the mixture, patting it on to make it stick. Put the pork in a shallow dish, cover, and refrigerate for 12 days, turning the belly over every 2 days. Liquid drawn from the meat by the salt may collect in the dish and does not need to be drained off. Pat the belly dry when the time is up and coat with a mixture of the spices and herbs, pressing them on so they stick (if the surface of the pancetta is already dry and un-sticky, moisten it with damp hands, then press the herbs and spices on). Using a skewer or thin-bladed knife, make a hole in a corner of each of the belly pieces and push a string through for hanging. Tie the string to form a loop and hang the pancetta, uncovered and with a dish underneath to catch any liquid or spices that may fall, in the back of your refrigerator, where the temperature is more stable, for 3 weeks. (I hang them from paper clips bent around the rod supporting the shelf in my fridge and they dangle there as if in a curing cave, all authentic and Old World, but if that doesn't work for you, pancetta can also be cured on a wire rack with the skin side down.) At that point, you can scrape off the spices and herbs and cut slices as needed, trimming the hard skin off only the part you are cooking with—leave the rest on there to protect the meat from overdrying. Depending on how quickly you use the pancetta, you can just leave it hanging. It does get quite hard after about 2 months, so if you won't use it all up by then, either freeze half, tightly wrapped, or give it away to a lucky, pork-appreciative friend.

BUTTERED PEAS WITH PANCETTA, LETTUCE, AND SAGE

At some point every spring, I just want peas for dinner. I want to sip some wine while we sit around and shell them, and then eat a luxuriously large bowl of sweet green peas. The meaty chew of pancetta, soft crunch of lettuce, and aromatic sage fill in any gaps.

Makes 6 servings

1 tablespoon cooking oil, olive or vegetable

3 ounces pancetta, cut into thin matchsticks

Leaves from 4 sage sprigs (about 20 leaves)

3 to 4 pounds peas, shelled (about 4½ cups)

3 or more tablespoons unsalted butter

Kosher or sea salt

1 small head romaine or butter lettuce

Heat a large skillet to medium and add the cooking oil, then the pancetta. Cook, stirring occasionally, until lightly browned, about 5 minutes. Tip off most of the fat, add the sage, and let it sizzle, stirring, for 30 seconds. Add the peas, butter, a good pinch of salt, and enough water to not quite cover the peas—about halfway up their little green bellies. Bring to a boil over high heat, lower to a simmer, and cook, stirring occasionally, while you cut the lettuce leaves across into thin strips. If it seems like too much lettuce, save some for another use. Taste a pea and when you think, *It just needs a half minute more,* it's time to add the lettuce. There should be some liquid in the skillet, but if the peas are completely awash, tip some out. Stir in the lettuce and add another pinch of salt. When the lettuce is wilted but still has crunch, it's done.

ARUGULA AND FENNEL SALAD WITH MINT, WHITE BEANS, AND CRISPED PROSCIUTTO

It had been nearly thirty years since the last time I saw Cesare Casella. The renowned Tuscan chef, transplanted to New York and now a prosciutto maker, stopped by Chez Panisse in my final months there with Patrick Martins, founder of Slow Food USA, Heritage Foods, and Heritage Radio Network, to talk ham. Because of a catastrophic fire at the Edwards Smokehouse in Surry, Virginia, Patrick had been left holding hundreds of hams that were destined to be cured there. Enter Cesare, who put his salt and magic on the homeless hams and many months later, there he was in the dining room with a breast pocketful of rosemary sprigs and a cutting board covered with slices of sweet, salty, rosy-red prosciutto.

I had followed Cesare's career ever since that evening so many years ago when I first stepped into his dreamy restaurant, Vipore, not far from the house where we were staying in the hills outside Lucca. Cesare greeted us with glasses of icy Prosecco and a plate of hot fried polenta covered with porcini mushrooms and made me an instant fan. Those were formative days for this young cook—Cesare, Vipore, porcini, the Tuscan landscape, all simmering me toward my decision to transition from an art career to a culinary one. Of course, Cesare knew none of this, and when I told him the story at Chez Panisse and thanked him for inspiring me, I think he might have gotten just a little bit misty.

"After that first time, we came to Vipore almost every evening for a drink at the bar. You and your family were so kind to us, and I remember the big fire you always had going under the grill, and I remember eating *tagliata di manzo* covered with herbs from your gardens."

"I'm sorry," he said, "but I don't remember. But tonight, when I call Mamma, I'll ask her. She'll remember you, Mamma remembers everyone." And he calls her every night!

He invited me to come back to Vipore, explaining that though he no longer runs the restaurant, he still has an apartment above it and we were all welcome. Until we do revisit those beautiful hills and inimitable aromas, this salad will have to do, evoking Tuscany with beans, Vipore's gardens with herbs and greens, and Cesare with prosciutto.

Makes 6 servings

2 cups cooked white beans, such as Italian butter or cannellini (see page 165), drained, liquid reserved

1 almond-size garlic clove, pounded (see page 6)

Good olive oil

Kosher or sea salt

6 thin prosciutto slices

½ teaspoon Dijon mustard

1 teaspoon red wine vinegar

1 teaspoon sherry vinegar

Freshly ground black pepper

1 small fennel head, green parts trimmed away, rinsed if needed

1 teaspoon lemon juice

3 handfuls arugula, washed and dried

Leaves from 6 mint sprigs, thinly sliced

Heat the oven to 325°F.

In a blender, combine the beans, half of the pounded garlic, 3 tablespoons olive oil, and a pinch of salt. Puree, adding just enough of the bean cooking liquid to make it go. Taste, adjust, and set aside.

Lay the slices of prosciutto on a wire rack placed atop a baking sheet (or directly on the baking sheet if you don't have a rack) and bake them until stiff, 12 to 15 minutes. Don't worry if they seem bendy—the slices will crisp as they cool.

Meanwhile, make the vinaigrette: In a small bowl, stir together the remaining pounded garlic, the mustard, vinegars, grindings of black pepper, a pinch of salt, and 3 tablespoons olive oil. Taste, adjust, and set aside.

Cut the fennel in half through the root end and then cut across into very thin slices, starting at the stem end and stopping when you get to the tough core. Put the fennel in a salad bowl and dress with the lemon juice and a pinch of salt. Set aside.

Spread the bean puree on a platter. Add the arugula and the mint to the salad bowl with the fennel, and dress with most of the vinaigrette and a pinch of salt. Toss well, taste, adjust and pile onto the platter with the bean puree peaking out. Arrange the prosciutto slices around the arugula, breaking them into pieces as desired. *Mangia!*

WARM SPINACH SALAD WITH BACON, EGG, AND SHERRY-SHALLOT VINAIGRETTE

Bacon-y salads that are served at my dream diner:

1. *Cold-snap-crisp iceberg wedge that involves creamy blue cheese*
2. *Wilty spinach with hot, twangy, mustardy dressing, lots of shallots, and chopped egg*

Go to this diner if you know where it is and send me a card. Till the postman comes, I'll be making warm spinach salad with bacon at home because it smells so vinegary good.

Makes 4 servings

3 eggs

1 golf ball–size shallot, minced or thinly sliced

1 almond-size garlic clove, pounded (see page 6)

Kosher or sea salt

Freshly ground black pepper

1½ teaspoons red wine vinegar

1 teaspoon sherry vinegar

1 big teaspoon Dijon mustard

½ pound tender spinach leaves

1 tablespoon cooking oil, olive or vegetable

2 or 3 bacon slices, cut into ¼-inch strips

Good olive oil, as needed

Hard-boil the eggs: Bring a small pot of water to a boil, slip the eggs in, and cook for 9 minutes for a set but not overcooked, choppable yolk. Cool, peel, chop (or push through a sieve or spider), and set aside.

In a small bowl, stir together the shallot, garlic, ¼ teaspoon salt, grindings of black pepper, the vinegars, and mustard. Set aside.

When you're ready to serve the salad, put the spinach in a large mixing bowl, preferably stainless steel. Sprinkle the chopped egg on top and season with salt and black pepper.

Warm a skillet over medium-low heat, add the cooking oil, then the bacon, and cook until it's the way you like it: soft, crispy, or in between. Add the shallot mixture and when the dressing is hot and bubbling a little, pour it over the greens and toss well. Taste for salt and acidity and adjust, adding good olive oil to temper the vinegar if needed. If the spinach seems as if it could use a little more wilting, hold the bowl over a burner briefly while you toss.

Serve warm, making sure that every plate gets some of the good stuff that's collected in the bottom of the mixing bowl.

ROASTED PANCETTA-WRAPPED ASPARAGUS WITH MUSTARD AND EGG

A pancetta-wrapped bundle is a happy bundle. The only trick here is matching thickness of asparagus stalk with thickness of pancetta slice. The thicker the asparagus, the longer to heat through, and so thicker pancetta is desired. For medium-thick to thick asparagus you want slices of pancetta that are a little thinner than the average bacon slice. For pencil-thin asparagus, the pancetta should be thinner still, but if that's not an option, just make bigger bundles and it'll work. You'll get it, and even if it takes a couple tries, well, is that so bad? I have also wrapped green bean bundles this way with tasty results.

Makes 6 servings

3 eggs

Kosher or sea salt

Freshly ground black pepper

½ almond-size garlic clove, pounded (see page 6)

2 teaspoons red wine vinegar

1 teaspoon Dijon or whole-grain mustard, or a combination

3 tablespoons good olive oil

1 large bunch asparagus (about 1¼ pounds)

Cooking oil, olive or vegetable

12 thin slices pancetta (thickness of a regular bacon slice)

¾ cup herb leaves picked from stems: chervil, tarragon, dill, parsley, or mint—solo or in combination

Bring to a boil a pot of water big enough to cook the asparagus in. Slip in the eggs and cook for 9 minutes. Cool and peel the eggs, then chop, grate, or push through a spider—I prefer the eggs to be pretty chunky. In a medium bowl, season the eggs with salt and pepper and set aside. Keep the water simmering.

Heat the oven to 425°F.

Meanwhile, make the vinaigrette: Mix the garlic, ¼ teaspoon salt, a few grindings of pepper, the vinegar, and mustard together in a small bowl or jar with a lid. Stir the olive oil into the bowl or add to the jar and shake. Set aside.

Snap off the tough ends of the asparagus and, unless they are thin as a pencil, peel the lower two-thirds of the stalk. Bring the water back to a boil, add salt till it tastes right (see page 8), then the asparagus, and cook until tender with just a little bite, 4 to 6 minutes. Drain and spread out on a baking sheet until cooled.

Sprinkle the asparagus with cooking oil and salt and turn with your hands to coat. Divide the spears into six piles and wrap each with 2 slices of pancetta, spiraling them around so that they're more sashes than belts. Roast until the pancetta is lightly browned and getting crisp, about 5 minutes.

Arrange on plates or a platter, splash the vinaigrette around, and sprinkle with the chopped eggs and herbs. Serve it.

GREEN BEANS AND PEPPERS
WITH PANCETTA, GARLIC, AND SAGE

BY VINE OR BY BUSH *(for the growers)*

There are farmers I have come to know,
through the green beans that they grow.
So I'd like to thank, as I'm departin'
a longtime grower, name of Martin.
And sunny Capay's morning fog
bringing fat Blue Lakes from Riverdog
and Terra Firma, or do I blunder?
Are they in fact Kentucky Wonders?
When then appear sweet haricots verts,
we drop our totes, we stop, we stare
at colors purple, green, and yellow
from Dirty Girl and Annabelle, O
Rattlesnakes! Romanos! Dragon Tongues!
Once topped and tailed and strings unstrung,
and cooked with garlic and pancetta:
I don't believe it gets much better.
Such verdant fruits of hers, of his
from pole, from field. Yes! Truly 'tis
a fool who tries to choose between
our favorite farmers of the bean.

Kosher or sea salt

1 tablespoon cooking oil, olive or vegetable

3 ounces pancetta, cut into thin matchsticks

2 medium size, tender, sweet red or orange peppers, such as Cubanelle, Gypsy, or Pimiento (about ½ pound), cored, seeds and veins removed, and thinly sliced

½ teaspoon red wine vinegar

2 tablespoons good olive oil

1 pound green beans, stem ends snapped off

2 almond-size garlic cloves, chopped

Leaves from 4 sage sprigs (about 20 leaves), roughly chopped

Bring a pot of water to a boil for the green beans. Add plenty of salt.

Meanwhile, warm a small skillet over gentle heat, add the cooking oil, then the pancetta, and cook until it's the way you like it: soft, crispy, or in between. Raise the heat to high and add the peppers and a sprinkle of salt. Stir and cook until the peppers are just wilting but still have crunch, about 5 minutes. Turn off the heat, stir in the vinegar and good olive oil, and keep warm for the green beans.

Taste the water to be sure it's salted right (page 8) and add the green beans. Stir once and while they are cooking, add the garlic and sage to the skillet over medium heat. Stir until it smells good but the garlic doesn't brown, then add the drained green beans when they are tender. Add a splash of water to slow things down in the skillet if the beans aren't done yet. Stir over high heat to bring everything together, taste, adjust, and eat, thinking about what rhymes with farmer.

GRILLED PANCETTA-WRAPPED FIGS SMASHED ON TOAST

People with fig trees know that when they are going full bore, loaded with fruit in late summer, smashed figs are a fact of life. Even if you are eating as many as you can and giving more away, it's hard to keep up, and things will get pretty jammy under that tree. This is a recipe inspired by, and to help remedy, the situation. These toasts are good just as they are with drinks, and are very nice as a first course or lunch alongside a salad of arugula, frisée, or lettuces.

Makes 6 servings

12 thin slices pancetta

12 ripe Ping-Pong-ball-size whole figs, or 6 larger figs cut in half through the stem

Cooking oil, olive or vegetable

Kosher or sea salt

Freshly ground black pepper

1 tablespoon chopped rosemary leaves

Six ½- to ¾-inch-thick slices good bread, each big enough to take 2 figs onboard

Good olive oil

Balsamic vinegar (optional)

Prepare a clean, hot grill.

Wrap the pancetta slices around the figs, coat them lightly with cooking oil, and sprinkle with salt, pepper, and the rosemary. When the grill is ready,

cook the figs, turning them to brown all sides. They should be very soft: When you fear that with any more cooking the grill will become their final home, they are done. Keep the figs warm while you grill the bread.

Drizzle the toasts with olive oil, smash 2 figs onto each, and drizzle sparingly with the balsamic vinegar, if using.

PIPERADE WITH PANCETTA AND BAKED EGGS

"Come over for barbecued eggs sometime," Dani said with a smile. "They're not fancy. It'll be brunch. With bacon," she added, laughing.

Dani and Will, aka the steel-drum and ukulele band Sister Exister, had just finished playing at the chicken coop dedication party where we met. As we talked about food and music, I realized that Dani was formerly known as Dan: Dan Leone, who, for nearly twenty years wrote "Cheap Eats," a beloved column in the *San Francisco Bay Guardian*. "Cheap Eats" was great because it was never just about the burrito shack or greasy Chinese place that was technically being reviewed. Dan would write about his friends and his chickens, his band's gigs, and his own transition. Eventually it became an alt-sports column about amateur women's boxing, kickball, pickup baseball, and bicycle hockey. Then in 2013, the column ended, and the *Guardian* did the same shortly after.

I missed "Cheap Eats" and now, here was Dani, its creator, serving me barbecued eggs! She scrambled and cooked them inside hollowed-out, bacon-wrapped sweet peppers—deliciously working the same pleasure points as this recipe for piperade with pancetta and baked eggs. The ingredients and technique are a little different, but the savor is the same.

1 almond-size garlic clove, pounded (see page 6)

¼ cup finely chopped parsley

¼ cup good olive oil

Kosher or sea salt

1 tablespoon cooking oil, olive or vegetable, plus more as needed

6 ounces pancetta, cut into thick matchsticks

1 medium yellow onion, thinly sliced

3 large red, orange, or yellow bell peppers, stem, seeds, and veins removed, thinly sliced

1½ teaspoons red wine vinegar

6 eggs

Delicious loaf of bread (optional)

Make the salsa verde: In a small mixing bowl, stir together the pounded garlic, parsley, good olive oil, and a pinch of salt. Taste, adjust, and set aside.

Heat a large skillet that can go in the oven to medium and add the cooking oil and the pancetta. Cook, stirring occasionally, until lightly browned, 5 to 7 minutes. Add the onion, bell peppers, and ½ teaspoon salt. If your pancetta is on the leaner side, you may need to add a tablespoon or two of cooking oil. Stir well to coat and cook, stirring occasionally, until both the onion and the peppers are very tender and sweet, about 20 minutes (at the 10-minute mark, heat the oven to 450°F). If needed, use a lid and/or a splash of water to keep things stewy.

Stir in the vinegar. Taste and adjust the piperade, then make 6 little divots in the mixture and crack an egg into each. Sprinkle the eggs with salt and put the skillet in the oven until the eggs are cooked the way you like them—6 to 7 minutes will yield a set white and soft yolk. Serve straight from the skillet with bread, if using, and the bowl of salsa verde to pass around and dab onto the eggs.

ROASTED TOMATO AND FENNEL SOUP
WITH BASIL, PANCETTA, AND AÏOLI TOASTS

I like to cook with concassé—peeled, seeded, and diced tomatoes—but I try not to say it that much: It's the kind of jargon that gives restaurant kitchens a bad rep. A bunch of guys barking out stuff like *mise!* (ingredients) and *chaud!* (watch out or I'll burn you) and *flavor profile!* (flavor) makes me nervous. If anyone starts with the *oui chef!* business, I'm out of there.

But for chunky summer pasta sauces (like the one for Penne alla Tunanesca, page 90), concassé is great. For soups and smoother sauces, the easiest and best way to deal with abundant ripe tomatoes is to roast them: half an hour or so in a hot oven and they are juicy, falling apart, smelling great, and ready to go into your sauce or soup. Also, the tomatoes don't have to be voluptuous beauty queens—for them, there are the BLT pageants of midsummer. Other times, roast those little tough-but-tasty numbers and make them into this PLT-inspired soup.

Makes 6 servings

1½ pounds ripe red tomatoes (Early Girls are great for this soup)

Cooking oil, olive or vegetable

Kosher or sea salt

1 medium yellow onion, thinly sliced

1 large fennel head, green parts and core removed, thinly sliced

½ teaspoon crushed fennel seeds

1 cup loosely packed basil leaves, plus a few more for garnish

3 garlic cloves, thinly sliced

6 thin pancetta slices (half the thickness of a bacon slice)

6 slices good rustic bread

3 to 6 crisp lettuce leaves (such as romaine, Little Gems, or even iceberg)

Aïoli (recipe follows; optional)

Heat the oven to 450°F.

Give the tomatoes a rinse, remove the stems (or not), halve them (or not), and put them into an oven-going skillet or roasting pan with ¼ cup oil and ½ teaspoon salt. Roast until very juicy and soft—smashable with the back of a spoon—about 45 minutes, stirring once or twice. Pass the tomatoes through a food mill to remove the stems, skins, and seeds, or just pluck out the stems and skins and leave the seeds.

Lower the oven to 350°F.

Heat a soup pot over high heat and add ¼ cup oil, then the onion, fennel, fennel seeds, and a teaspoon of salt. Stir, lower the heat, and cover the pot. Check and stir after a few minutes, letting water from the lid drip back into the pot to keep things steamy. Lower the heat if there is any browning going on, and re-cover. Cook like this until very tender, about 15 minutes. Roughly chop the basil leaves and add them and the garlic to the pot. Raise the heat to high and stir for a minute, then add the roasted tomato puree and 2 cups water. Bring to a boil, then lower to a slow simmer. Cook, stirring occasionally to prevent sticking, for 20 minutes. Taste and correct as needed for salt. Sometimes, if it seems too acidic, I will spin some, or all, of the soup in a blender—it helps the onion and fennel do their sweet and smooth thing.

While the soup simmers, lay the pancetta slices out on a baking sheet and, setting a timer for 5 minutes, put them in the oven. Check the pancetta and continue baking, resetting the timer for a minute at a time, until crisp. Set the pancetta aside and bake the slices of bread until toasty-brown. Set aside.

Slice the reserved basil leaves and the lettuce leaves into thin strips. Taste the soup and adjust—does it need a cup more water to take it from sauceland to souptown? Ladle the hot soup into warmed bowls. Spread the toasts with aïoli, if using (or just rub a clove of garlic over the toasts and drizzle generously with good olive oil), and set afloat. Sprinkle the lettuce and basil strips over the toasts, crumble on the pancetta, and serve.

AÏOLI

1 egg yolk

1 almond-size garlic clove, pounded (see page 6)

1 cup light olive oil (spicy olive oil can make aïoli bitter)

1 teaspoon red wine vinegar

1 teaspoon lemon juice

Whisk the egg yolk and pounded garlic together in a small bowl—the size matters here: the oil whisks into the egg yolk more readily in a snug vessel. It doesn't make sense, but somehow a mortar and pestle also works. Begin to add the oil drop by drop, stirring all the while. Drip slowly and stir quickly until the yolk begins to hold the oil and thicken, about ¼ of the way through. Now you can pour the oil in a little quicker, in a stream, but you cannot stop stirring. Keep going and at about the ½ cup mark, the emulsion tends to get a little too thick, so add a teaspoon of water. Use all the oil, and then stir in the vinegar and lemon juice. If the aïoli looks very shiny and bouncy, add a little more water to smooth it out. Taste and adjust.

SALSA RUSTICA WITH EGG AND PANCETTA

Though the pork here is pancetta, this is basically bacon and egg sauce and you could, of course, make it with bacon if that's how you feel. Small amounts of finely chopped oregano, marjoram, rosemary, thyme, or sage can be added as available. Spoon salsa rustica over grilled bread, grilled or roasted vegetables, roasted potatoes, sautéed greens, sliced tomatoes, boiled green beans, or cauliflower . . .

Makes about ¾ cup

2 eggs

Kosher or sea salt

Freshly ground black pepper

1 tablespoon cooking oil, olive or vegetable

3 ounces pancetta, cut into thin matchsticks

1 almond-size garlic clove, pounded (see page 6)

¼ cup finely chopped parsley

3 tablespoons good olive oil, plus more if needed

Hard-boil the eggs: Bring a small saucepan of water to a boil, slip in the eggs, and cook for 9 minutes. Cool and peel, then chop, grate, or push through a spider—I prefer the eggs to be pretty chunky. In a medium bowl, season the eggs with salt and pepper and set aside.

Meanwhile, warm a small skillet over medium-low heat, add the cooking oil, then the pancetta, and cook until it's the way you like it: soft, crispy, or in between. Drain and set aside both the pancetta and the fat.

Add the pancetta, garlic, parsley, olive oil, and a pinch of salt to the chopped eggs. Mix well, taste, and consider adding a tablespoon more of the olive oil or a tablespoon of the reserved pancetta fat. Spread everywhere, as if it were good news, which it is.

Variation: More good news, this from the salty sea: Replace the pancetta with 8 anchovy fillets, drained and chopped or pounded to a paste. Keep the eggs in there, or don't.

GREENS WITH BIG CHUNKS OF BRAISED PANCETTA AND GARLIC CLOVES

Of course the pieces of pancetta can be as big as you want, but I like to cut them so that each person gets 2 or 3 meaty chunks. It takes a bit of time to get to nearly falling-apart tender when cut this way, but it's worth it. The greens, too, should be well done—cancel your kale massage appointment; this is more of a dark and tender, deep-flavored Rolfing treatment.

If you need some seed ideas for how to eat these greens, other than all by their succulent selves, here are three: toast, beans, eggs—not necessarily all together, not necessarily not.

1 tablespoon cooking oil, olive or vegetable

8 ounces pancetta, cut into 12 chunks

12 garlic cloves, whole, unpeeled

½ cup dry white wine

Kosher or sea salt

2 bunches kale, collard, or mustard greens, stems removed and leaves roughly chopped

Heat the oven to 450°F.

Heat a large, oven-going skillet to medium and add the oil, then the pancetta. Cook until lightly browned, turning the pieces to get all the sides, about 5 minutes. Add the garlic and wine, raise the heat, and bring to a simmer. Add enough water to nearly cover the pancetta, bring back to a simmer, and put the skillet in the oven, uncovered. Turn the oven down to 325°F and cook until very tender, about 1 hour, checking occasionally and adding more water if it has all evaporated. Skim off some of the fat if it seems excessive. You can slip the garlic skins off when cool enough to handle, or let eaters do it themselves.

Meanwhile, bring a pot of water to a boil, add salt till it tastes right (see page 8) and then add the greens, stirring and pushing them down into the water. Cook at a slow boil until tender—cooking time depends on the greens you are using, so taste a piece to determine doneness.

Drain the greens, add them to the skillet on the stovetop, and bring to a simmer. Cook slowly for at least 10 minutes to bring the flavors together, or longer if the greens still need some time.

BUCATINI ALLA GRICIA

Once I worked with someone who was mostly quite sensible, insisting on a kind of simple, divine, loveliness that was easy enough to grasp until, suddenly, it wasn't. You thought you got it, had your watershed moment and lovely divinity was at hand, only to look up and see that someone had raised the bar, or lowered it, or angled it—it sometimes became hard to even find the confounded bar, which made one want to *find the bar*!

Finally, I began to understand that everything I made was being compared to a memory, an ideal from the past, a pleasure probably had in Paris, or Provence. I like sweet memories, particularly when they are my own, but it is notoriously hard to compete with the time when someone and her cute boyfriend were twenty, high on hot baguettes and cool rosé, wandering through France and feeding each other sweet moules frites in every seaside bistro. No boyfriend will ever again be that cute, no mussels that sweet. Flavors, sights, and scents can combine and amount to significant moments, and significant moments are good to honor, but not reproduce. It's folly to try to chase that nectar.

Or is it folly not to? Why shouldn't Kathleen and I sit together in the sun at the edge of the sea, as we did in Sicily, rinsing just-plucked urchins in the cold water and then eating them right there, with glasses of cold Prosecco? We should—not to redo *that* time, but to be there *this* time. Of course, the great thing about adventuring in food is that you can adventure right here at home, inspired by, but not defined by, your sweet and salty memories.

Can I replicate the luxuriously greasy strands of bucatini alla gricia I slurped up in a dirty-delicious Trastevere restaurant years ago? The short answer is no. The long answer? A whole hog lifetime of trying. The secret ingredient that is getting *me* closer? Pork lard. Optional.

Makes 4 servings

Kosher or sea salt

1 pound bucatini

3 tablespoons rendered pork lard or cooking oil, olive or vegetable

4 ounces guanciale (cured pork cheek—can be replaced with pancetta or, reluctantly, bacon), cut into little strips

¾ cup grated Pecorino Romano, more for serving

Freshly ground black pepper

Bring a large pot of water to a boil and add salt till it tastes right (see page 8) Add the bucatini, stir a couple times in the first minutes, then occasionally. When the bucatini is halfway done (after about 5 minutes), heat a skillet over medium and add the lard or oil and the guanciale or pancetta. Cook, stirring and lowering the heat if it gets too sizzly, until the meat is softened and transparent. If the bucatini isn't done yet, add a splash of cooking water to the skillet and keep warm.

When done, reserve a little of the cooking water, drain the bucatini, and toss it in the skillet with the grated cheese and plenty of black pepper. Mix well, tasting and adjusting the sauciness with oil and/or splashes of the reserved cooking water. Pass more Pecorino Romano and the peppermill at the table.

BRUSSELS SPROUTS WITH PANCETTA, GINGER, AND CILANTRO

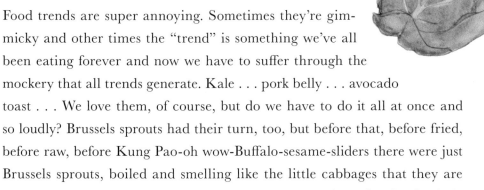

Food trends are super annoying. Sometimes they're gimmicky and other times the "trend" is something we've all been eating forever and now we have to suffer through the mockery that all trends generate. Kale . . . pork belly . . . avocado toast . . . We love them, of course, but do we have to do it all at once and so loudly? Brussels sprouts had their turn, too, but before that, before fried, before raw, before Kung Pao-oh wow-Buffalo-sesame-sliders there were just Brussels sprouts, boiled and smelling like the little cabbages that they are and that we loved. We still like to come home sometimes for simple, fork-tender, rolled in butter comforts, but we have evolved and enjoy also the the luxury to play with ingredients of all types and from faraway places, as in this recipe.

Makes 6 servings

1¼ pounds Brussels sprouts, trimmed and halved through the stem end

Cooking oil, olive or vegetable

Kosher or sea salt

4 ounces pancetta, cut into thick matchsticks

2 teaspoons minced ginger

½ cup chopped cilantro stems and leaves

1 lime or lemon (optional)

Heat the oven to 425°F.

In a mixing bowl, toss the Brussels sprouts with 2 tablespoons cooking oil, 2 tablespoons water, and 1 teaspoon salt. Spread on a baking sheet and roast until browned and tender all the way through, about 30 minutes, but taste to be sure (and add more salt if needed). Sprinkle with a tablespoon or 2 of water if the Brussels sprouts are browning too much before getting tender.

Meanwhile, heat a large skillet to medium and add 1 tablespoon cooking oil and the pancetta. Cook, stirring occasionally, until lightly browned, about 5 minutes. Tip off some of the fat if you feel you need to. When the Brussels sprouts are done, add the ginger and cilantro to the skillet with the pancetta over medium heat. Stir for 30 seconds, then add the Brussels sprouts and stir well. Taste, adjust, and consider squeezing in lime or lemon juice—as I sometimes do.

BACON-WRAPPED POTATO GRATIN

One time, for my birthday, my friend Tamar Adler cooked bacon for me. Just that: a very big pork belly, a fatty feast for a bunch of friends. If you've ever had pork belly slow-roasted just right, so that the lean, meaty part is tender and the rest is browned and mmmmmelty, you know how it can be, how you might overindulge. Luckily, it was my birthday, so there were plenty of drinks to neutralize the fat. Or something. Tamar remembers that there was salad and artichokes; I remember only that pork belly. But since this book is about using small amounts of things like pancetta as seasoning, Tamar's recipe doesn't really fit. (But . . . you *could* season a pork belly generously with salt, black pepper, and cracked coriander and fennel seeds today, pop the belly into a roasting pan and into a 425°F oven tomorrow, turn the heat down to 325°F after 30 minutes, and roast it until a knife slips in and out easily, about another 1½ hours. Call friends for dinner and think about the incredible sandwich you can make tomorrow.)

Still, sometimes too much is just enough, so this is my attempt at pushing the bacon envelope by actually *making* a bacon envelope and stuffing potatoes inside it. This gratin is never going to be lean, but the trick to keeping it sane is using thinly sliced bacon, which, if your store doesn't have it, can be simulated by stretching regular-sliced bacon: Lay a slice on a cutting board and use a chef's knife, tilted so that the blade is nearly parallel to the board, to slide over the bacon, pressing down enough to squeeze it thin, but not so hard that it tears.

Makes 6 servings

¾ pound thinly sliced bacon (see note above)

2 pounds medium to large yellow potatoes, such as Yellow Finn, Yukon Gold, or German Butterball

Kosher or sea salt

Freshly ground black pepper

Leaves from 6 thyme sprigs, chopped

Line a 9-inch cast-iron skillet or 7 × 10-inch casserole dish with the bacon slices, allowing enough overhang so that they will fold up to cover the potatoes completely. Depending on the shape of the vessel you are baking in—round, square, rectangular—there are a number of ways to make this happen, and part of the fun is figuring it out. Remember that the bacon will shrink as it cooks, so overlap the slices slightly.

With a sharp knife or a mandoline, carefully cut one of the potatoes into very thin slices—about ⅛ inch—and lay them in rows that overlap to make a single layer. Sprinkle lightly with salt, pepper, and the thyme, and repeat with the remaining potatoes until the dish or skillet is full. Use your hands to press down on the potatoes and settle them into place, then fold the bacon over to cover the top. Fold your hands over your own belly and chuckle with contentment.

Cover with foil and bake until a thin-bladed knife meets no resistance at the center of the gratin, 30 to 40 minutes. Uncover the gratin and return it to the oven to bake until nicely browned, an additional 10 to 15 minutes.

Let cool for 10 minutes, then cut into portions with a sharp knife.

ESCAROLE SOUP
WITH PANCETTA AND GARLIC TOAST

Before I had the kind that Bob Cannard grows on his farm in Glen Ellen, California, I thought escarole was just for soup. Bob's escarole—pale, sweet, tender, and absolutely saladable—changed that. In fact, it was so good that I started to miss the old tough green escarole, the kind that, when combined with a few white beans, strips of pancetta, and garlicky toasted bread, makes a real nice soup. Now I buy two heads, dressing the inner leaves with a punchy dressing—like almond and anchovy dressing (page 81) or bacon and sherry-shallot dressing (page 127) for a salad today, and saving the outer leaves for soup tomorrow.

Makes 3 quarts, about 12 servings

1 tablespoon cooking oil, olive or vegetable

6 ounces pancetta, cut into thick matchsticks

1 medium yellow onion, diced small

1 carrot, diced smaller than the onion

Kosher or sea salt

1 tablespoon roughly chopped rosemary leaves

3 garlic cloves, thinly sliced or chopped

Crushed red pepper flakes

8 cups homemade chicken stock or water

½ cup white rice, any kind really

1 escarole head (or the outer leaves of 2 escarole heads, see headnote), roughly chopped

3 eggs

¼ cup grated Parmesan (optional)

A garlic clove to rub the optional toasts with (optional)

Tasty toasts, one per bowl (optional)

Good olive oil

Heat a soup pot to medium and add the cooking oil, then the pancetta. Cook, stirring occasionally, until lightly browned, about 5 minutes. Lift the pancetta out of the pot and set aside. Pour off some of the fat if it seems excessive (or leave it—you can always decide to skim it off later) and add the onion, carrot, and ½ teaspoon salt. Stir occasionally over low heat until soft, about 15 minutes, adding splashes of water if needed to avoid over-browning. Add the rosemary, garlic, and red pepper flakes and stir for 30 seconds, then add the stock and rice. Raise the heat to high and bring to a boil, stirring once or twice to prevent the rice from sticking. Lower the heat and simmer gently for 5 minutes. Stir in the escarole and continue cooking until the rice is done, about 10 minutes, but taste to be sure and to adjust for salt.

When you're ready to serve, raise the heat to bring the soup to a lively bubble. In a mixing bowl, whisk the eggs with the Parmesan, if using, and a pinch of salt. Pour the egg mixture into the bubbling soup while you stir to create golden threads. Serve hot—

over toasted, garlic-rubbed bread or not—and doused with plenty of good olive oil.

Variation: Instead of threads of egg, you can create a thicker, creamier effect by intro-ducing the egg mixture more gently: turn the heat off under the soup and when it stops bubbling, slowly whisk a ladleful into the bowl of beaten eggs to temper them. Repeat with two more ladlefuls, then whisk the egg mixture into the pot. Do not bring back to the boil.

RUMAKIS

My mom cooked for our family pretty much every night, except when there was company coming over for dinner in the dining room on a Friday night. On those nights, my sister and brother and I got sticks: frozen fish sticks and French's potato sticks from a pop-top can. We loved Stick Dinner; we'd eat it with ketchup on trays in front of the TV and get a can of mandarin orange slices and some Nilla Wafers for dessert. Weeknights, Mom had a solid line-up of family favorites that included pork roast, spaghetti, and a very tasty meat loaf, and, for weekend company, Chicken Marquis and Veal Marsala.

I thought she was adding to her hit list when I smelled what Mom had going in the broiler one Friday night. A dinner party was in the works, ice was rattling in glasses, and through the ladies' perfume I was getting a sweet and smoky whiff, caramel-y, and with a dark, mysterious tang. We were meant to stay out from underfoot on these nights—unlimited TV!—but I had to know. Keeping low, below the cigarette-smoke layer, I slipped past stockinged and slacked legs and into the kitchen. Mom turned from the stove when she heard me come in: Even in stealth mode, I couldn't resist sliding in my socks on the linoleum floor and had collided with a chair, but I wasn't busted—Mom, in good spirits, earrings, and an apron over her nice dress, smiled at my question.

"Rumakis," she said with a light, vodka tonic twinkle and a little laugh that should have aroused suspicion, but I smelled bacon, and something

better than bacon. I wasn't aware that there was such a thing. "Want to try one?"

"Yes, please!" I blurted, then gobbled.

Betrayal is sometimes slow in coming, a deferred wounding that only makes itself fully felt later, with reflection and perspective. My Friday-night massacre took only as long as it takes for teeth to cut through a slice of bacon. For beneath it lay a nugget of chicken liver the texture of treachery and the flavor of bitterness and blood.

Mom didn't see the look of horror on my face. She'd turned back to arranging her treason-on-a-toothpick offerings for the unsuspecting lambs chatting over their cigarettes and Scotch and I ran back to the TV room, making good use of a napkin on the way and with a harrowing story of evil to tell my brother and sister.

Rumakis, I now know, *are* as delicious as they smell: little tiki roll-ups of chicken liver and water chestnut in bacon, marinated in soy sauce, ginger, and brown sugar and broiled or grilled on toothpicks. Like at Traitor Vic's, I mean Trader Vic's.

Makes 12 rumakis

8 ounces chicken or duck livers

Kosher or sea salt

Freshly ground black pepper

1 tablespoon finely grated or minced ginger

1 tablespoon whole coriander seed, toasted (see page 14) and coarsely ground

Crushed red pepper flakes to taste

1 teaspoon brown sugar

2 tablespoons soy sauce

1 tablespoon sherry or Shaoxing wine

1 tablespoon cooking oil, olive or vegetable

12 slices water chestnuts (about half an 8-ounce can)

4 scallions, trimmed and cut into 12 equal lengths

4 slices bacon cut into 12 equal lengths

12 wooden toothpicks

Trim any connective tissue or discolored bits from the livers and cut as needed into 12 somewhat equal pieces. Season lightly with salt and black pepper— remember, the soy sauce and bacon will add saltiness as well.

In a medium bowl, whisk together the ginger, coriander, red pepper flakes, brown sugar, soy sauce, and sherry until the sugar dissolves. Set 2 tablespoons of the marinade aside to use later as a sauce and place the livers in the remaining marinade. Stir to coat well and marinate for 15 minutes at room temperature if cooking them now, or for an hour or two in the fridge if cooking later. Bring to room temperature before cooking.

Lift the livers from the marinade and wrap each one, along with a slice of water chestnut and a length of scallion, in a piece of bacon and secure with a toothpick. Discard the used marinade. Cook the rumakis under a hot broiler or on the grill until the liver is just cooked through, about 5 minutes. Spoon the reserved marinade over the rumakis and serve hot.

Flexitarian variation: Wrap mushroom caps instead of livers in bacon. Or, um, tofu.

CELERY GRATIN WITH BACON

Funny thing about this recipe: The ingredients are so ubiquitous that you can practically shop for them at the convenience store and yet it's also kind of exotic and as suave as a silk purse. And if you don't have the fresh herbs, you can just crank in lots of black pepper instead (but don't substitute dried herbs, please). Or grate that cheese end that's been bothering you. Some toasted and crushed cumin or fennel seeds? Sure. All of the above? Easy now.

BTW, the word "convenience" comes from the Latin, meaning assembling, agreeing. So that's nice. Maybe we all need to spend more time at those stores, convening and reminding them to stock good beer and real food.

Makes 4 servings and is easily doubled

2 cups whole milk

4 tablespoons (½ stick) unsalted butter

3 tablespoons all-purpose flour

Kosher or sea salt

Cooking oil, olive or vegetable

2 to 3 slices bacon, cut across into little strips

1 celery head, leaves removed, stalks separated, rinsed, and cut into 1-inch chunks

Leaves from 3 to 4 thyme sprigs, chopped

Freshly ground black pepper

Pour the milk in a small saucepan and heat not quite to a boil.

Meanwhile, in a medium saucepan, melt the butter over low heat. Add the flour all at once and whisk it into the butter with a pinch of salt. Adjust the heat so that the roux is bubbling mildly and whisk for 3 minutes. The roux should stay pale. Raise the heat to medium and ladle in a little milk, about a quarter cup, whisking constantly. Whisk until the milk is completely mixed in, and then add another ladleful. Again, whisk until it's all the same consistency. Repeat, whisking all the while, always waiting to add more milk until the previous addition is fully incorporated. When the sauce has the thickness of heavy cream, whisk in all the remaining milk and raise the heat to medium-high. Switch from the whisk to a wooden spoon, or rubber spatula that can take the heat, and continue stirring, being sure to cover every spot of the bottom of the pan to prevent scorching. Stir and stir until the béchamel just begins to simmer. Once simmering is confirmed, turn the heat to the lowest setting, stir a minute more, and cover incompletely. Continue to cook, stirring occasionally, for 10 minutes more. Taste, correct for salt, and hold warm and covered.

While the béchamel is cooking, heat the oven to 425°F and oil the inside of a casserole dish that the celery will fit in. Bring a pot of salted water to a boil for the celery.

Cook the bacon with a little oil in a small skillet until it's the way you like it: soft, crispy, or in between. Drain, or don't, and set aside.

When the water is boiling, taste it for salt and then add the celery. Cook until tender, about 8 minutes, but taste it at 6. When the celery is done, drain it, saving a little water to adjust the béchamel thickness, and toss it in a large bowl with the thyme, grindings of black pepper, the bacon, and béchamel sauce. Stir well and splash in a little cooking water to thin if it seems too clumpy.

Spoon into the casserole and bake until bubbling in the middle and lightly browned, about 15 minutes. Carefully run the dish under the broiler if you want more color on top.

Nice with just a green salad or alongside grilled vegetables or chicken.

Variation: When the gratin is nearly done, sprinkle with 2 cups of Toasted Bread Crumbs (page 50) and bake a few minutes more.

OYSTERS BAKED WITH CELERY ROOT, CREAM, AND PANCETTA

My friend Bobby would buy cream in cartons of a size ordinarily associated with milk for his version of oyster bisque. Admirable for its simplicity—it was literally oysters cooked in cream, nothing else—it was ridiculously rich. I had to talk him into adding even black pepper and chives, and though we eventually worked in some onions, potatoes, and stock, it took some convincing.

Keeping Bobby's freaky fatty flame alive, I converted his bisque to this proportionately appropriate, lighter, but no less delicious (pancetta!) baked oyster appetizer, like a spoonful of soup in a shell.

Makes 2, 3, or 4 servings, depending on appetites and what else you're having

12 oysters

1 small or ½ large celery root, peeled

Kosher or sea salt

1 tablespoon cooking oil, olive or vegetable

2 ounces pancetta

Leaves from 4 thyme sprigs, chopped

½ cup heavy cream

2 tablespoons unsalted butter

Freshly ground black pepper

Rock salt (optional)

1 lemon

Shuck the oysters, tipping off and saving any liquor. Loosen the meat from the shells, leave it in the deeper shell half, and refrigerate until ready to bake. Discard the other shell halves.

Cut the celery root into very small dice, the size of small peas. Bring ½ inch of water to a boil in a skillet, add a light pinch of salt (the pancetta and oysters themselves are salty) and the celery root, and cook until tender, 3 to 5 minutes. Drain and set aside.

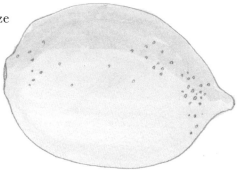

Heat the oven to 450°F.

Warm the oil in the same skillet and add the pancetta. Sizzle gently until it turns translucent and begins to lightly brown, about 5 minutes. Tip out some of the fat if there's a lot. Add the thyme, sizzle it for 10 seconds, then add the cream and any reserved oyster liquor (be careful to leave behind any sand or shell bits that may have settled). Bring to a simmer, add the celery root, and cook until slightly thickened, like chowder. Stir in the butter and a few grindings of black pepper.

Arrange the oysters on a baking sheet or in a large, oven-going skillet or flat casserole. A base of rock salt can help keep the oysters level, but you can balance them without it, too. Spoon the cream mixture onto the oysters and bake until hot, about 10 minutes.

Squeeze lemon juice over the oysters and slurp them up as soon as they won't burn your lips.

WARM BREAD WITH LARDO
AND BLACK TRUFFLE

"Lardo again?!" my dad asked, signalling with an Italian gesture that he was still a good sport and with an improving vocabulary. *"Ancora?"*

I was traveling around Tuscany with my dad and he was right; everywhere we went it seemed like lardo season. I love the stuff—cured pork back fat, like bacon, though not smoked and without the lean—but Dad was appalled.

"Sounds," he grimaced, "and looks, just like . . . like lard! They're eating lard on bread here? Is that okay for the heart?"

"Dad . . ." I started.

"What's the word for 'butter'?" he said, holding some focaccia and looking around for the waiter.

"I'll have yours," I said and reached for his plate, folded a translucent strip of pure pork goodness into my mouth, and clutched at my chest, the sweet fat instantly clogging an artery.

"Molto funny." Dad's Italian was getting better.

Several trattorias and lardo refusals later, we stopped during a Chianti downpour at the famous Antica Macelleria Cecchini. I had met the butcher, Dario, years before when he visited Chez Panisse and wanted my dad to see his purple cowboy boots and hopefully hear him recite some Dante. Plus, we were hungry and I knew Dario always had wine and snacks laid out for his customers.

We hurried in out of the rain and nearly went down on the spotless and slippery wet terrazzo floor. Steadied by glasses of wine, we were offered a choice of crostini topped with either lardo or salsiccia crudo.

"*Salsiccia,*" I told Dad when he turned to me for help, "means sausage, and crudo is raw."

"Raw sausage?!" he mouthed at me with a look of confused shock, then turned to the butcher, "Lardo for me, *per favore.*"

Makes 6 servings

1 black truffle, or 12 fried sage leaves (recipe follows)

Kosher or sea salt

Good olive oil

12 half-inch-thick slices of baguette

12 thin slices of lardo

Heat the oven to 425°F.

Slice the black truffle very thinly and dress in a small bowl with a pinch of salt and oil to coat. Cover and set aside in a warm place till the oven is hot. Arrange the bread slices on a baking sheet and top each with slices of truffle (or fried sage leaf) and dab around the oil. Cover the truffle slices with pieces of lardo and bake just until the lardo turns translucent, about 1 minute. Pass around the toasts to have with drinks or serve alongside a green, herby salad.

Variation: Use pancetta if you can't find lardo: Cut the bread into longer, thicker slices and spiral-wrap with pancetta sliced a little thicker. Bake until the bread is crisped on the outside but still soft inside. Great with a green salad, a bowl of beans, or a plate of eggs.

FRIED SAGE

Cooking oil, olive or vegetable   Kosher or sea salt

Sage leaves, picked from stems

In a small saucepan or skillet, pour at least ¾ inch of oil, enough for the herbs to swim around in. Heat the oil to 325°F or until shimmery, not smoking, and a leaf dropped in sizzles enthusiastically. Fry the sage leaves, and when the sizzling has nearly stopped and the green color has darkened but not browned, scoop them out and onto a paper towel to drain. Sprinkle with salt.

You may want to go ahead and fry the rest of your sage leaves—for later—they will last, covered tightly and refrigerated, for at least a week.

CREAMY WHITE BEANS
WITH PANCETTA AND ROSEMARY

My friend Scott makes chairs. He builds other things, like large, interactive public art installations, visionary tree houses, and sleek cruiser skateboards shaped from luxuriously dark walnut wood, but over the twenty or so years that we've been friends, Scott has designed and made chairs. When he mentioned over dinner that he was designing the chairs for a popular new restaurant and asked if anyone had an idea for a good café chair, another guest piped up right away. The vision that eight-year-old Greyson described, a potato chip–shaped seat with a curved, wire back and padded armrests, didn't say café comfort to me, but I had no original ideas of my own to offer, the old bentwood standards suiting old, bent me.

But I believe in visionaries in general, and Scott and Greyson in particular, and I look forward to sitting in their chairs. Inspired by such a playful lack of complacency, I turned to white beans with pancetta. Is there a more easy chair of a dish than a bowl of tender white beans with rosemary, not *rosemary!*, a couple of chunky strips of pancetta, and a slick of good olive oil? *Holy fagioli!* Maybe there is! What if I were to put a couple ladlefuls of the cooked beans in a blender with a little pancetta, some garlic, a discretion of

rosemary, and a handful of stale bread for a bean-boosting panade to be stirred back in? Get comfortable.

Makes 2+ quarts or 6 to 8 servings

3 cups dried white beans, such as Italian butter or cannellini

Kosher or sea salt

As many of these aromatics for the beans as you have: ½ small onion, 1 small carrot, ½ celery stalk, a garlic clove, a bay leaf, a small whole or partial tomato, a thyme sprig or two, a few parsley stems

2 tablespoons cooking oil, olive or vegetable

4 to 6 ounces pancetta (depending on your indulgence), cut into little strips

1 almond-size garlic clove, pounded (see page 6)

Scant ½ teaspoon chopped rosemary

2 ounces stale bread, de-crusted and torn into pieces

Look over the dried beans for any small rocks or dirt clods. Rinse the beans, put them in a large bowl, and cover them with plenty of cold water. Leave them overnight on the counter, or if the weather is hot, in the fridge.

Next day, drain and rinse the beans and put them in a large pot covered with fresh water by a couple of inches. Place the pot over high heat, add salt till it taste right (see page 8) and the aromatics, and bring to a boil. Lower the heat to a simmer and skim off any foam with a ladle. Taste the water for salt, add more if needed, and cook, stirring infrequently but checking more often to see that you don't need to add water, until very tender, 1½ to 2 hours.

Meanwhile, warm a skillet over medium-low heat, add the cooking oil, then two-thirds of the pancetta, and cook over gentle heat until it's the way you like it: soft, crispy, or in between. Set aside.

Remove the aromatics from the bean pot and discard them. Transfer about a cup of beans in their liquid into a blender with the remaining pancetta, the pounded garlic, chopped rosemary, and bread. Blend until smooth, adding more bean liquid if needed, then return the puree to the pot and add the cooked pancetta strips. Bring back to a simmer, stirring to prevent sticking and burning. Taste, adjust, get yourself a bowl, and sit down in a nice chair.

acknowledgments

With gratitude to salt—and tree, land, and sea—for nuts, fatty bellies, and tasty little fishes.

And to

Kathleen, Henderson, Milo, and Liam—the best mouths to feed.

My mom and dad and sister and brother, for your love, laughs, and support.

Hungry storytellers—you make dinner much better.

Mary Jo Thoresen—thanks for the nutty ideas.

Lori Wood and Kelly Sicat at Montalvo Center for the Arts, Lee Hudson and Cristina Salas-Porras Hudson at Hudson Ranch, and Fred Reid, for nice quiet places to write.

Cassie Jones and Sharon Bowers, for knowing a good thing or three when they hear it.

Everyone at William Morrow, including Anwesha Basu, Anna Brower, Suet Chong, Ryan Cury, Lynn Grady, Tavia Kowalchuk, Rachel Meyers, Mumtaz Mustafa, Liate Stehlik, and Kara Zauberman.

universal conversion chart

Oven temperature equivalents

250°F = 120°C	350°F = 180°C	450°F = 230°C
275°F = 135°C	375°F = 190°C	475°F = 240°C
300°F = 150°C	400°F = 200°C	500°F = 260°C
325°F = 160°C	425°F = 220°C	

Measurement equivalents

Measurements should always be level unless directed otherwise.

⅛ teaspoon = 0.5 mL

¼ teaspoon = 1 mL

½ teaspoon = 2 mL

1 teaspoon = 5 mL

1 tablespoon = 3 teaspoons = ½ fluid ounce = 15 mL

2 tablespoons = ⅛ cup = 1 fluid ounce = 30 mL

4 tablespoons = ¼ cup = 2 fluid ounces = 60 mL

5⅓ tablespoons = ⅓ cup = 3 fluid ounces = 80 mL

8 tablespoons = ½ cup = 4 fluid ounces = 120 mL

10⅔ tablespoons = ⅔ cup = 5 fluid ounces = 160 mL

12 tablespoons = ¾ cup = 6 fluid ounces = 180 mL

16 tablespoons = 1 cup = 8 fluid ounces = 240 mL

index